THE EMBODIED PLAYBOOK

THE EMBODIED PLAYBOOK

Writing Practices of Student-Athletes

J. MICHAEL RIFENBURG

UTAH STATE UNIVERSITY PRESS
Logan

© 2018 by University Press of Colorado

Published by Utah State University Press
An imprint of University Press of Colorado
245 Century Circle, Suite 202
Louisville, Colorado 80027

 The University Press of Colorado is a proud member of
the Association of University Presses.

The University Press of Colorado is a cooperative publishing enterprise supported,
in part, by Adams State University, Colorado State University, Fort Lewis College,
Metropolitan State University of Denver, Regis University, University of Colorado,
University of Northern Colorado, Utah State University, and Western State Colorado
University.

∞ This paper meets the requirements of the ANSI/NISO Z39.48-1992 (Permanence of
  Paper)

ISBN: 978-1-60732-688-5 (paperback)
ISBN: 978-1-60732-689-2 (ebook)
https://doi.org/10.7330/9781607326892

Library of Congress Cataloging-in-Publication Data

Names: Rifenburg, J. Michael, 1982– author.
Title: The embodied playbook : writing practices of student-athletes / J. Michael
  Rifenburg.
Description: Logan : Utah State University Press, [2017] | Includes bibliographical refer-
  ences and index.
Identifiers: LCCN 2017025371| ISBN 9781607326885 (pbk.) | ISBN 9781607326892
  (ebook)
Subjects: LCSH: College athletes—Education—United States. | English language—
  Rhetoric—Study and teaching (Higher)—United States. | Learning strategies.
Classification: LCC LC2581 .R54 2017 | DDC 796.04/3092—dc23
LC record available at https://lccn.loc.gov/2017025371

The University Press of Colorado gratefully acknowledges the generous support of the
University of North Georgia toward the publication of this book.

Front cover concept and illustration by Bradley Huff

To
Albert Jackson Dennen

*Granddad, thanks for not letting me play football but
always making me talk football.*

CONTENTS

FIGURES

ACKNOWLEDGMENTS

My near decade-long research into student-athlete writing practices began by chance. As an incoming MA student at Auburn, I was asked by Michelle Sidler to coteach an FYC class largely populated by first-year student-athletes. As the hot Alabama summer stubbornly gave way to autumn, I watched highly decorated football players excel on the playing field and struggle in our writing class. And I wondered why. Certainly, there may have been motivation factors and issues of focus and balancing the life of a Division I student-athlete in a prominent athletics program. But I felt there was something more that caused such dissonance between the cognitive space of sport and school. So my reading, writing, and thinking began. After I attended my first CCCC in 2008, I wrote an e-mail message to Chris Anson introducing myself and my research and asking to learn more about the talk he gave at CCCC that year. We bounced e-mails around one July morning, and, looking back, it was the first time someone who wasn't on my MA committee and to whom I wasn't married expressed interest in and encouragement for my work. I still have the e-mails. Thanks, Chris. I presented my work a year later for the first time at a graduate-student conference hosted by Ohio State. John Duffy was in the audience and introduced himself. He asked for a copy of my talk, and I was thrilled. Thanks, John. Thanks to Marty Townsend for introducing me to the NCAA president, Mark Emmert, and the former athletic director of Missouri, Mike Alden, at CCCC in St. Louis and for showing me that one can make a career out of (academically) caring for student-athletes.

Much thanks to Julie Huff at Auburn, who hired me to supervise mandatory student-athlete study hours and introduced me to the academic side of college sports. To Kevin Roozen, for listening to my ideas and reading disjointed but passionate seminar papers and an MA thesis on student-athlete literacy. To Tom Nunnally, who helped me with my gnarled prose and then invited me to his backyard to shoot pistols. And to John Bolton, Miriam Clark, Anna Riehl, and former officemate Caroline Wilkinson.

I was fortunate to continue my work at Oklahoma. Much thanks to Jaye Amundson, Katie McIntyre, and Brooke Clevenger, staff members in athletic academic services, and to the athletics director, Joseph Castiglione, for teaching my graduate class on college sports and sitting down for an interview. Much thanks to Michele Eodice and Moira Ozias at the OU Writing Center for offering me a space to think about my ideas and, more important, to learn with other writers. I can't think of a more welcoming space. Thanks to Catherine Hobbs, Kathleen Welch, and Susan Kates for reading and encouraging my work. To Alan Velie for not tolerating florid sentences, and to Vince Leitch for helping me navigate the publication process. To my graduate-student friends Jerry Stinnett, Shannon Madden, Tara Wood, Ted English, and Rachel Jackson. And, of course, to Chris Carter.

At the University of North Georgia, the athletics department welcomed a curious researcher. Thanks to Margaret Poitevint, Lindsey Reeves, and Chris Faulkner. Thanks to Jon Mehlferber and Kayla Mehalcik for help with the images. To my good friend, Brad Huff, for the cover image. Much thanks to my Friday writing group, where we listened to Tycho and forced words across the screen.

A handshake with Michael Spooner, too. I pitched him the idea for this book on a patio in Tampa, Florida. From that initial meeting, he has helped shaped this book immensely. There is a reason Utah State University Press was the first press I approached with my book. And Michael is a large portion of that reason.

I started this book with three living grandparents and no children of my own. At the end of this writing journey, I have one living grandparent and three children. The words on the page are what you see, but family allows me to get the words onto the screen. This book began in earnest when my oldest, Maddux, was an infant; I received a contract on this book in late August, and the next day my wife told me she was nine weeks pregnant; I finished editing the first draft of this book on Darcy's second birthday; I submitted the second round of revisions on my wife's birthday. My wife, Amy, understood why I was still in my office even though it wasn't a teaching day. My children reminded me that Mario and Minnie Mouse are quite enjoyable and that there is a world, a beautiful world, beyond my computer screen, beyond my research notes, books, and writing. My in-laws allowed me to move my wife from Georgia to Alabama to Oklahoma and back again to Georgia. My parents encouraged my literate development from an early age; one of my fonder memories is learning to read by flipping through *Calvin and Hobbes* with my dad. That's how I first learned the word *tyrant*.

Finally, around the time I graduated from Georgia College with my BA, I visited my grandparents in Lafayette, Louisiana. One evening, my grandfather, an old high-school football coach at Mater Dei High School in California, fell asleep in his armchair watching football. My eyes wandered to his bookshelf. I saw a thin volume forcefully wedged between signed copies of Robert Penn Warren's *All the King's Men* and Joseph Heller's *God Knows*. It was *The Corinthian*, an undergrad research journal published by Georgia College. My first article, a clunky analysis of the poetic rhythm of Tennyson's "Charge of the Light Brigade," was bookmarked in the journal. Even as I type these words many, many years later, I'm still not sure how my grandfather reasoned that my sophomoric (literally and figuratively) work should sit alongside Warren's and Heller's. But I find myself constantly heartened by such lofty praise.

I went to visit him at Lafayette General Hospital as I was nearing completion of this book. It was a dark October night. His once large, powerful frame was hidden behind bed sheets, wires, tubes. His vision was spotty at best. He reached out a hand to shake mine, and I silently marveled at the strength still left in a hand that once gripped a football. He asked about my drive to Louisiana and then about my book. I mentioned it was finished, and he gave a silent nod of approval. I drove off into the warm Cajun night and didn't see him again. Thanks for the nod and the handshake and the love of football and life, Grandpa. I'll save you some boudin and Guinness.

THE EMBODIED PLAYBOOK

1

INTRODUCTION
Studying the Writing Practices of Our Student-Athletes

> *491,930 student-athletes competed in NCAA sponsored sports in 2016–2017.*
> —2016–2017 NCAA Sports Sponsorship and Participation Rates Report

As origin stories are critical to how we understand and undertake our work, I start with two origin stories fueling my inquiry into the writing practices of our student-athletes.

Origin story 1: It is my first summer as an MA student at Auburn University, and I am responsible for supervising mandatory study hours for incoming first-year student-athletes. We are in the first floor of the library. Outside, it is a hot, sticky Alabama summer; inside, it is cold, quiet. A handful of student-athletes work on a paper for their success-strategies class, which I am coteaching with a counseling psychology professor. I am walking around checking on progress. I walk up to a highly recruited wide receiver I will call Trey. The success-strategies paper is his first college paper. He is writing it on Notepad, a clunky, plain-text editor included in all versions of Windows since the initial launch of Windows in 1985. I suggest using Word. Trey's face shows confusion. Talking with him, I learn about his lack of access to technology in his high school and home; I learn about his struggles with writing; I learn about his excitement over being able to start the computer, log on with his new student ID, locate Notepad, and write; I learn of his decorated high-school football career. I leave Trey to Notepad and his writing. My head spins over the palpable disconnect between Trey's academic and athletic preparedness. Trey leaves Auburn for academic reasons less than a year later.

Origin story 2: Again, the setting is Auburn during my time as an MA student. Researching student-athlete literate practices for my thesis, I gain access to a group of first-year football players, the wide receiver in origin story 1 among this group. They are all taking a first-year writing

DOI: 10.7330/9781607326892.c001

course I am coteaching with a more experienced PhD student. Once the Institutional Review Board approves my research, I sit down to interview a first-year defensive lineman. Let's call him Jason. I ask Jason how he learns the team's complex plays. He tells me a story about being in the locker room early in the season when he voiced frustration aloud with the amount and complexity of the plays. An upperclassman walked over to him. The upperclassman took the cushions off the locker-room sofa and arranged them on the floor in the pattern of a common play Auburn runs. Moving the cushions around the floor, the upperclassman walked Jason through the play's nuances. Jason learned the play and contributed to Auburn's success on the field that season.

Two years later, I graduated and began progress toward a PhD at the University of Oklahoma. In my living room in Norman, Oklahoma, with my one-month-old son in my arms, I watched Auburn win the national championship by defeating the University of Oregon under the lights in Glendale, Arizona. Another student-athlete I cotaught in that first-year writing course kicked the game-winning nineteen-yard field goal. I watched him celebrate, my former student. He ran around, his arms held high, his mouth spread in jubilation, his gold necklace dancing against his shoulder pads. Jason, too, celebrated with his teammates. But Trey, Jason's former teammate and my former student, wasn't there to celebrate. He had left the school before the season started.

These two origin stories propelled my teaching, research, and service over the past decade at two Division I schools and one Division II school. One a story of struggle, one a story of success. At the time, I knew there was something deeper to these stories. One student-athlete struggled to connect his bodily literacy to the academic classroom, while another leveraged his bodily literacy in unique ways to solve a complex cognitive problem: how do I learn hundreds and hundreds of plays? Bodily literacy and knowing through the body is at the heart of these two origin stories. Unfortunately, since bodily literacy does not often figure into traditional conceptions of academic literacy, composition instructors and the programs and people under which they labor do not often privilege bodily literacy in writing-intensive spaces like an FYC classroom or a writing center. This local dismissal of bodily literacies gives rise to global dismissal in that higher education stakeholders often understand the one-half million student-athletes, student-athletes like Trey and Jason, through a cognitive-deficit model: here is what they *cannot* do, here is what they *don't* know. This misleading model drives mainstream media headlines, provides fodder for campus conversations, social media posts, and listserv threads. I understand I take a quick leap of logic from the classroom to mainstream media headlines decrying student-athlete academic performance, but in the following pages, I argue compositionists can better work with student-athlete writers by understanding their prior knowledge, a prior knowledge honed through bodily engagement with text and through writing practices that privilege the body as a central mode of meaning making.

I don't naively believe better pedagogical practices of working with student-athlete writers will wash away over a hundred years of stains in the relationship between athletics and academics—stains most clearly visible in the fabric of Division I schools. I soon map this century-long relationship between school and sport but do believe, naively or not, that composition studies has always looked for how to work better with the many unique student populations we are trained and committed to serve. I do believe that despite all the challenges our field endures and has endured, we stay committed to whoever is in our classrooms. I do believe Adam Banks's (2015) words during a powerful moment in his chair's address at the 2015 Conference on College Composition and Communication gathering in Tampa—possibly the most powerful speech I have heard in person. With a rising crescendo, he stressed that we—composition teacher-scholars—"served anyhow" (271). No matter the budget deficits, marginalization, and ostracization by and from other disciplines, we "took care of our students anyhow" (271). I do believe engaging with a unique population in a manner of being slow to speak and quick to listen yields reciprocal benefits. The immediate results of knowing our student-athlete writers better may be negligible in term of the national landscape of NCAA athletics. But compositionists play the long game; we serve anyhow.

One year after these two origin stories, I was in New Orleans and walking the halls of my first Conference on College Composition and Communication. Overwhelmed by the sheer size of the conference, my eyes caught the Digital Archive of Literacy Narratives booth. Volunteers working the booth capture brief video literacy narratives from conference attendees. These narratives populate an open-access digital archive for instructional and research purposes. A volunteer approached me and invited me to provide one. Into my head popped the origin stories that had altered my view of literacy, learning, higher education, access, college sports. But I couldn't talk about them just yet. I couldn't give voice to how my view of literacy specifically changed. Again, I knew there was something there. Something I couldn't quite put my finger on. All I could have talked about for the video narrative was what I had witnessed and that what I had witnessed made me say *hmmm*. I declined and walked on.

A decade later, I am ready to give voice to what I learned that hot, sticky Alabama summer night in the library and during my interview with the defensive lineman Jason.

I am ready to talk about the writing practices of our student-athletes.

To ground this book, I focus specifically on football and men's basketball because, as I argue throughout these pages, the student-athletes competing in these sports operate within a highly discursive space most evident in how they engage with scripted plays. I define *scripted plays* in the next chapter; however, to start, I understand scripted plays as multimodal texts created, implemented, and even curated with the public performing body as the central mode of meaning making. Other sports use scripted plays, but for football and men's basketball, most, if not all, of the bodily public action is undergirded by scripted plays. In articulating the writing practices of our student-athletes, then, I begin with a focus on plays. Plays are textual gateways into understanding how student-athletes know.

Starting with this premise, my proceeding inquiry is threefold: What are plays and what do they do? How do student-athletes learn plays? And, finally, how can we better teach student-athletes based on these findings? These three questions constitute the aims of the following chapters and culminate in a single query that has dogged me since my time working with first-year student-athletes at Auburn: how do student-athletes know?

In *The Embodied Playbook: Writing Practices of Student-Athletes*, I seek to understand better the Treys and Jasons many of us teach. According to the *NCAA Sports Sponsorship and Participation Rates Report* (National Collegiate Athletic Association 2017b), 491,930 student-athletes competed in NCAA -sponsored sports during the 2016–2017 academic year. The total student-athlete population has grown 19 percent over the last decade. I can only imagine the numbers will continue rising. The close to one-half million student-athletes have a unique story to tell. Their story will illuminate not only how we approach literacy instruction and theory but also how we approach the most lucrative extracurricular appendage of US higher education: college sports. First, however, we need to look behind the headlines and the ESPN news blips about the wonders and worries of college sports to listen and learn. I can't help but wonder whether Trey, like Jason, might have stayed at Auburn, might have celebrated the national championship with his teammates if I, or the larger composition studies community, knew more about how student-athletes know. . More important, he might have graduated. Certainly many factors drive retention—still, what if?

THE ANTAGONISTIC RELATIONSHIP BETWEEN
ATHLETICS AND ACADEMICS

In this book, I take this nagging personal question and broaden it to speak to the many institutional and community stakeholders who work with our student-athletes. My personal *what if* question then becomes *how do student-athletes know?* And how can we better support their writing development based on what they know? Though my focus is on student-athletes' writing practices, I am aware that when I step into the waters of student-athletes and academics, I am also stepping into rolling waves of frustration at college athletics for soaring expenditures, countless scandals, and what many perceive to be either a blatant disregard for or an insouciant approach to academic standards. I acknowledge these soaring financial expenditures and scandals and touch on the historically antagonistic relationship between school and sport later in this section.

According to *Forbes*, the five most lucrative college football teams are all worth more than $100 million each, with the University of Texas at Austin leading the way at $131 million (Smith 2014). I spent four years working in athletic academic services at the University of Oklahoma. The athletics department operates with a roughly $100 million self-sustaining annual budget. Other sports are financially viable because of the revenue generated by football. According to 2012–2013 records, the Oklahoma football team brought in 34 percent of the revenue, with an expense of roughly 25 percent of the budget (University of Oklahoma 2013). At the Division I level, men's basketball programs also commonly operate in the black even though the sport does not generate such high dollars. *Forbes* reports that the University of Louisville has the most valuable team at just under $40 million, with the University of Kansas coming in second. Kansas generated $14.5 million alone from ticket sales (Smith 2015).

Broadcast rights also drive the revenue for football and men's basketball though administrators are often hesitant to disclose specific numbers. The SEC—a conference that claimed seven straight football national championships between 2006 and 2012—partnered with ESPN in 2014 to launch the SEC Network. One year after the launch, the SEC announced a record distribution of $455.8 million divided among the fourteen conference schools. Then-commissioner of the SEC, Mike Slive, would not say how much of that revenue stemmed from the ESPN partnership; however, the previous year, the SEC distributed just $292.8 million. The SEC isn't the first to nuzzle up to a network in hopes of a richer payday. Notre Dame has long worked with NBC, which holds broadcast rights for Notre Dame football. This deal brings in around $20 million annually (the exact number is hard to locate because Notre Dame, a private school, does not always disclose financial records). Texas launched the Longhorn Network with ESPN in 2011; the Big Ten started the Big Ten Network. The NCAA, too, generates the majority of its revenue from television deals. According to a 2015 independent consolidated financial report disclosed by the NCAA, the NCAA generated over $776 million from "television and marketing rights fees," the majority coming from the Division I men's basketball tournament under contract with CBS/Turner (*National Collegiate Athletics Association and Subsidiaries* 2015). These are the numbers that jump out at us and that we remember when talk turns to college athletics even though more student-athletes compete in Division II and III—not high-dollar and high-profile Division I sports—and even though more athletics programs have modest budgets and operate in the black than have budgets near $100 million and operate in the red. In this book, I move from big-time Division I athletics at the University of Oklahoma to small-scale Division II athletics at the University of North Georgia. I move from an athletics program with an annual self-sustaining budget of roughly $100 million to an athletics program with a budget of roughly $3 million supported, in part, by mandatory student fees. College athletics takes on many forms across US higher education, and I want to be sensitive to the nuances of each program while also seeking to understand better how our student-athlete writers know and engage with text. However, I will say the soaring expenditures of sustaining a successful athletics program are realities affecting the everyday work of all stakeholders in US higher education. Like many, I am disheartened to read of mandatory student fees used to sustain floundering athletics departments, as is the case at Rutgers and other schools.

But I don't wade into a debate regarding the presence of college sports on our campuses. That debate is currently underway by scholars across various disciplines and is one certainly worth following. I tell a different story. I want to focus on the student-athletes who are already on our campuses, in our classrooms. I embrace Patricia Bizzell's (2014) powerful assertion that at the heart of composition studies is a desire to know who our students are (442). I want us to know our student-athletes. To know our student-athletes, we need to know their writing practices and broader literate practices.

I write aware of the task before me. Through nearly a decade of talking about my ideas at conferences, in journals, during hallway conversations, over coffee and other drinks, I'm aware many readers are indifferent to or outright hostile toward the uniquely US idea that an institution of higher education would funnel millions of dollars toward a game for students to play and fans to watch. I'm right there with those readers.[1] Faculty are largely frustrated, baffled, incensed with, or ignorant of the presence and even need for college sports in higher education. These mixed but generally negative reactions to college sports on the part of faculty are steeped in historical tradition. Though Isocrates (1929) in his fourth-century BCE text *Antidosis* argued for the inclusion of a liberal arts education because it would fuse the mind and the body, historian of ancient Western education H. I. Marrou (1982) points out that when the Romans adopted Greek education, they jettisoned athletics (and music, oddly enough) from the curriculum. We see the remnants of such a decision today as public schools in times of tightening budgets are more inclined to drop PE and music than math and social studies. Yet sport bubbled up again in US higher education during the middle of the nineteenth century at the same time the abstract ideals of bettering oneself through education were codified into the rapid proliferation of brick-and-mortar colleges and universities. The presence and need for college sports on our campuses is strange indeed and, yes, may even vitiate the foundation of US higher education, which is and should be academics. Though I direct attention to how student-athletes engage with plays and do not descend into arguments for or against the presence of college sports on our campuses, sliding into activity theory just for a moment helps remind us that the objectives/motives of college sports (to generate income, to win games, to brand a university) cannot be separated from the tools (the plays, the players, the stadium, the coaches) used to reach these objectives/motives. So, yes, in a sense, when I talk about the tools of basketball and football, when I talk about the text in which these student-athletes engage, I am indirectly talking about the larger motives of college sports and the larger issues giving rise and continuing to give rise to the prominence of college sports on our campuses, sometimes to the detriment of learning. In this section, then, I offer a brief overview of our turbulent history with college sports, not to accuse or excuse college sports but to erect the complex stage on which the writing practices of our student-athletes are performed.

Historian of education John R. Thelin (2004) writes that college sports were initially student-run extracurricular endeavors (178) free from the shackles of presidents, administrators, and boosters. Students organized the first football game between Rutgers and Princeton in 1869. Students at Michigan in 1881 coordinated road games in New England, and the team squared off against Harvard, Princeton, and Yale in the span of a week. In 1883, five years before Yale hired an official head coach and eight years before Princeton did, New York City was caught up in the thrill of a Thanksgiving match-up between Yale and Princeton. College-sports fervor engulfed the eastern half of the United States.

Just seven years after the Yale-Princeton match-up, two important decades began in the history of US higher education. Thelin points to the period between 1890 and 1910 as the time when the "American public became fascinated with undergraduate collegiate life" (Thelin 2004, 157), which in turn led to a growing awareness of and interest in college sports.[2] One result of the public's growing interest was what Thelin describes as the "transformation" of "the prototypical athletic association" through hiring athletic directors and coaching staffs (178). No longer coached by players, football hired official head coaches: Michigan in 1891, Chicago in 1892, Rutgers in 1895, and Princeton in 1901. The move toward professionalization dramatically altered the landscape of higher education. In his chapter titled "The Rise of Football," historian of education Frederick Rudolph contends, "Therefore, when the apparatus of athletics grew too large and complex for student management; when the expenditure of much time and much money was required in the recruiting, coaching, feeding, and care of athletic heroes; when, indeed, all these things demanded a more efficient and perhaps more subtle touch, the alumni jumped to the opportunity which student ineffectiveness and faculty indifference gave them" (Rudolph 1968, 382–83). Out of the hands of the students and of faculty disinterested in the extracurricular activities of their students, athletics blossomed, aiding in the marketing, branding, and financial bolstering of a university. Universities adopted colors proudly worn by supporters. Mascots, some of which were fearful (the Lions of Columbia, the Wolverines of Michigan) and some of which were humorous (the Purple Cow of Williams College, the Sagehen of Pomona College), were enlisted to personify the schools.[3] Fans displayed the orange and black of Princeton and the blue and white of Yale during the annual Yale-Princeton football game. The writer of a December 1893 *New York Times* article "The Orange above the Blue" estimated the crowd that year to be twenty-three thousand, larger than an average crowd at a typical NHL or NBA game today.

Powerful men reigned over the newly transformed college-sports enterprise. Walter Camp, Yale head coach from 1888 to 1892, diverted monies from smaller-revenue sports, such as swimming and gymnastics, to football. Through these clever—some might say devious—tactics, Camp deployed an "entrepreneurial strategy that allowed a coach and athletics director to gain leverage over both student groups and academic officials" (Thelin 2004, 179).[4] At the University of Chicago, Amos

Alonzo Stagg, a disciple of Camp's, became athletic director in 1892. Stagg procured himself a tenured faculty position, an administrative appointment as athletics director as well as football coach, a departmental budget exempted from customary internal review, and a direct line of reporting to the president (Thelin 2004,179).[5] On a more innocuous level, in 1893, Harvard created a salaried graduate manager of athletics in charge of the entire athletics program, leading Rudolph to assert that "this widely copied university office institutionalized alumni voice in athletic affairs and added an important new dimension, and problem, to college and university administration" (384).

Shady decisions by people like Stagg unsettled university presidents. President Harry Garfield of Williams College said in 1908, "Here [at Williams College] . . . there is grave danger of departure from the essential idea of a college as distinguished from an institute of physical culture" (Lucas 1994, 178). Administration at Cornell looked for ways to rein in college sports by "insist[ing] that games be played on college grounds and that players be bona fide students in good standing" (Bragdon 1967, 212). Harvard's president, Charles Eliot, however, pushed for banishment of football perhaps more for the sheer brutality of the sport than its impact on academics.[6] In 1892, he decried the "foolish and pernicious expenditures on sports" (Lucas 1994, 178). Eliot did not support self-regulated athletics programs. "It is childish," he declared, "to suppose that athletic authorities which have permitted football to become a brutal, cheating, demoralizing game can be trusted to reform it" (Smith 1990, 206). Nevertheless, football stayed.[7] Eliot could not bolster enough support.

University presidents sounded warning bells regarding athletics. Yet, many people in the United States believed a university's mission was to field a football team (Rudolph 1968, 387), a sentiment many share today. Pastors cut sermons short on Sunday to make time for the "big-game" (Lucas 1994, 177). Athletics departments witnessed rising profit margins. As president of Princeton, Woodrow Wilson said, "Princeton is noted in this wide world for three things: football, baseball, and collegiate instruction" (Zimbalist 1990, 7). The popularity of college sports, particularly football, led to rising profit margins for athletics departments. In 1928, Yale's athletic association reported a gross revenue of $1,119,000, with a net profit of $384,500 (Rudolph 1968, 389).[8]

Muckraker journalism of the early twentieth century drove the progressive era and social reform. The meatpacking industry underwent substantial reform following the publication of Upton Sinclair's *The Jungle* in 1906 (interestingly, the same year the NCAA formed), and

John Dewey reimagined a child's psychological development. The growing big-business practices of college sports were susceptible to these waves of reform. In 1929, the Carnegie Foundation released one of the first comprehensive accounts of intercollegiate athletics. Titled *American College Athletics* and prepared by Howard J. Savage, the detailed 347-page report become "the canon . . . for reform proposals and policy analyses about the place of intercollegiate sports in American colleges and universities" (Thelin 1994, 13). The report focused largely on players' safety, hygiene, and conduct and rules on the playing field, with only "some attention . . . paid to the bearings of college athletics upon the principles and practice of education" (3). The report garnered widespread media attention, but even though Savage worked for the Carnegie Foundation for the Advancement of Teaching, he did not focus on ensuring athletics would fall under the academic purview of a university. Rather, he focused on, among other things, the size of a playing field.

Now, in the early years of the twenty-first century, college sports are a dominant force on many college campuses. The NCAA governs college sports from its headquarters in Indianapolis. This powerful organization is wealthy. According to an independent auditor's consolidated financial report, the NCAA maintains over $900 million in total assets. Here's a disturbing recipe being prepared right now: mix the academic scandals ripping across the college-sports landscape with these gratuitous NCAA monetary resources, then stir in an era of intense financial austerity experienced by academic units in which the idea of a public— that is, a *publicly funded*—university is almost laughable, and we have a recipe for a tension-filled relationship between school and sport, which is reaching a boiling point. A December 2011 issue of the *Chronicle of Higher Education* screamed the following headline across the front page: "What the Hell Has Happened to College Sports? And What Should We Do About It?" Though the *Chronicle* is not hesitant to promulgate a rhetoric of excess through shocking headlines or images on its covers, the headline denounced the growing chasm between athletics and academics, the increase of scandals in college sports, and the general unrest among academics regarding the place of college sports on campuses of higher education.

Up to this point, the *Chronicle* generally spoke on the financial aspects of athletics programs. This December 2011 issue is different. It speaks to a deeper, more pressing challenge: the mercurial relationship between school and sport, which causes a divide at once rhetorical and material. This *Chronicle* issue signals a pivotal shift in the relationship between athletics and academics through a bold headline, with close to one-fourth of the issue devoted to the topic and with commentary by writers such as Frank Deford, basketball Hall of Famer Oscar Robertson, and the late president emeritus of the University of North Carolina system William C. Friday. Faculty, the stewards of a university, are not only concerned with pointing out what many perceive to be a gross level of revenue and expenditures in times of financial austerity. Faculty also often position athletics as a cancer rapidly metastasizing through the body of a school as evidenced by myriad recent incidents: a former assistant football coach at Penn State accused of sexual assault, the FBI's probing a point-shaving scandal at Auburn, a freshman basketball player at the University of Oklahoma taking money from a financial advisor, several TCU football players arrested in a police sting for drug possession with intent to distribute, and Louisville basketball coaches hiring escorts for recruits.. All these incidents took place after 2010 and at prominent schools, schools with a tradition of athletic success.

The scholastic side of college sports is just as bleak: football player Dexter Manley, who graduated from Oklahoma State, admitted in 1989 to the US Senate Subcommittee on Education that he was illiterate until his thirties; former Auburn football player James Brooks and former Creighton basketball player Kevin Ross give similar narratives. On December 28, 2008, Mike Knobler of the *Atlanta Journal-Constitution* wrote a front-page article detailing the discrepancy between the SAT scores of student-athletes at fifty-four public universities and nonsports students at the same universities. In 2012, Brad Wolverton of the *Chronicle of Higher Education* published a front-page piece on Memphis football player Dasmine Cathey. The piece comes complete with a powerful pull quote: "[Cathey] could barely read three years ago. How is this U. of Memphis student just three classes away from a degree?" (Wolverton 2012). Taken together, such a sampling illustrates the common disturbing narrative when considering college sports, particularly high-profile and high-dollar college sports, and higher education.

Yet all these student-athletes were matriculated at large Division I institutions. Aware of the rampant cognitive-deficit model surrounding student-athletes' academic ability, the NCAA has conjured up and implemented a host of formulas designed to track a student-athlete's academic progress. The Academic Progress Report, Graduation Success Report, Degree-Complete Award Program, Academic Success Rate, Eligibility Center, Path to Graduation, and many other initiatives and matrices work to illustrate to all stakeholders in US higher education that the NCAA is foremost invested in educating student-athletes.

Recently, the NCAA announced postseason bans for teams with poor APR scores and, as it proudly touts on its website, directs over $2.7 billion annually toward athletic scholarships. Through this money and through initiatives and matrices, student-athlete graduation rates are rising across divisions. Nevertheless, the NCAA cannot escape the shadow of Dexter Manley, James Brooks, Kevin Ross, and Dasmine Cathey because it is hard to understand why college sports (a fully professionalized, entrepreneurial, big-business, and uniquely US endeavor) are a component of higher education. Historically and contemporarily, the two are strange bedfellows, indeed.

Fields such as education and sociology have spoken to the tension between school and sport often and with passion. Bearing eye-catching titles about the scandal-ridden endeavor that is college sports, these analyses generally depict college sports as a sinful enterprise, anathema to the academic mission of higher education.[9] And groups such as the Knight Commission, the Coalition on Intercollegiate Athletics, and the Drake Group have authored concrete proposals for needed academic reform. But the constant theme since the mid-nineteenth century is that individual and collective drumbeats fail to marshal substantial change.

As I reflect on this brief overview of college sports from the first football game in 1869 to the 2012 *Chronicle* feature story on Memphis football player Dasmine Cathey, I understand why readers may approach *The Embodied Playbook: Writing Practices of Student-Athletes* with reticence or hostility. College sports and academics, more times than not, it seems, struggle to coexist, and academic departments often pay the penalty. Yet, I also can't help but notice a thread woven into the early part of this history influencing the challenges we face today and coloring how readers may approach my argument: overall faculty indifference to the crystallization of college sports. In his autobiography, Amos Alonzo Stagg pointed toward faculty indifference as a contributing factor to the "evils that have beset the game" (Stagg and Stout 1927, 176): "Most of the evils that have beset the game from time to time have been the direct result of student and alumni management, but a large portion of the blame belongs on the faculty doorstep. The students and alumni ran athletics because the faculty members had been too superior to concern themselves with such juvenilia. Their indifference was described, without overstatement at the time, as 'the crime of the faculties'" (Stagg and Stout 1927, 175, 176). Stagg's perspective is intriguing because of his ethos. Hired to run the athletics department at the newly formed University of Chicago in 1892, Stagg facilitated not only the growth of college football across the country from a motley assembly of male student groups into a coalition of teams, but, at Chicago, he also coached the baseball and basketball team, taught classes, and led campus construction efforts. A quick scan of his biography reveals a startling number of innovations and contributions across the sporting world: he invented the indoor batting cage and the headfirst slide in baseball. He was a member of the Olympic committee from 1906 to 1932 and designed troughs for overflow water in swimming pools. Edwin Pope (1955) provides a bulleted list of Stagg innovations such as the huddle, the lateral pass, awarding letters to players, adding numbers to players' jerseys, and, most related to the study of this book, writing the first book on football with diagrams with Minnesota's Dr. Henry Williams in 1893, after only one year at Chicago (232). Today, Stagg's legacy lives on in the Division III football championship game named the Stagg Bowl.

Serendipitous timing spurred Stagg's innovations and contributions. He worked at Chicago, a university founded in 1890 through the work of the American Baptist Education Society coupled with a magnanimous $35 million donation by John D. Rockefeller. Chicago undertook a novel approach to higher education. In embracing characteristics of the German and English university model, the university divided itself into colleges, engaged the community through lectures and evening and summer classes, and operated on a twelve-month calendar. Chicago began in an era of increasing academic specialization, which often resulted in faculty assuming a more insular perspective and focusing solely on disciplinary concerns. Such is the perspective at many schools today. Yet, Chicago faculty were involved in the lives of their students outside the classroom and committed to ensuring the proper role of athletics in the ecology of higher education. As Stagg wrote of Chicago, "There is no danger at Chicago of athletics getting out of bounds; that was taken care of at the outset by providing rigid faculty control and direction" (173). True to Stagg's declaration, Chicago dropped football in 1939—less than fifty years after the school's founding. As Stagg argued, "A college with brains and courage, however small, does not need to hire a squad of mercenaries to wear its uniform" (174). Chicago found other ways beyond sports to market the university and, in the face of the rising success of its athletics program—football won two national championships, and halfback Jay Berwanger was the first recipient of the Downtown Athletic Club trophy (now known as the Heisman Trophy) given to the best college football player—football was eliminated.[10]

Chicago is an isolated case of faculty and administrator involvement in early college sports. My reading of histories of college sports and higher education leads me to believe faculty across disciplines were disinterested in what students did outside the classroom. Such disinterest is understandable. As Robert Connors offers, professor/student relationships were discordant at best prior to 1850: "For students of most colleges before 1850, the faculty had one clear definition. It was the enemy" (Connors 1997 47). Connors reports that between 1800 and 1875, students rebelled against faculty at many prominent universities: "Stonings of faculty houses and other minor acts of violence were too common to catalogue" (47). Rudolph writes that the president of Oakland College was stabbed to death (Rudolph 1968, 97–98). Against such a backdrop, it is understandable that faculty would show indifference toward students' extracurricular activities. Through coeducation and other changes to higher education, the faculty/student animosity soon eased. However, even when presidents and the public did begin to consider the dangers of college sports, faculty did not become involved in crafting the 1929 Carnegie report, the first comprehensive report calling for the reform of college sports.

In the latter part of the twenty-first century, faculty groups such as the Coalition on Intercollegiate Athletics formed in hopes of reforming college sports. Established in 2002 by James W. Earl at the University of Oregon, the faculty-led COIA started as a grass-roots campaign among faculty senates in what was known then as the Pac-10 conference in hopes of giving faculty a voice in college sports. Earl connected with Bob Eno at the University of Indiana, and the COIA grew nationally. Partnering with other governing bodies, such as the Faculty Athletics Representative Association, the Association of Academic Advisors for Athletics, and the American Association of University Professors, the COIA positioned itself at the center of the debate surrounding intercollegiate athletic reform through policy papers, speeches at national conventions, and a presence in publications such as the *Chronicle of Higher Education* and *Inside Higher Ed.* The COIA is a recent faculty response to what many perceive to be an ever-growing chasm between athletics and academics. Faculty voice in college sports has been sorely absent in previous reform undertakings, but faculty need a voice if there is to be lasting change. Unfortunately, faculty indifference toward college sports morphed into faculty cynicism. I found strained relationships between the athletics department and many academic units at the two Division I schools where I worked. Athletics departments grow distrustful of academic departments; academic departments grow distrustful of athletics departments. Internecine squabbles arise. This cyclical reaction and infighting scholastically and socially harms the student-athletes and results in separate services for student-athletes at many schools, particularly Division I schools. Unsure of how best to implement vague NCAA mandates directed toward academics, and distrustful of academic departments, many athletics departments isolate themselves and their student-athletes from the academic side of a campus. But such vague mandates, though baffling and frustrating, are in the best interests of those committed to offering quality student-athlete writing support.

On January 22, 2015, two former student-athletes sued the NCAA and UNC for failing to provide quality education. In the one hundred-page class-action complaint (*McCants, Rashanda, and Devon Ramsay v. The National Collegiate Athletic Association and The University of North Carolina at Chapel Hill* 2015), Rashanda McCants, a former women's basketball player, and Devon Ramsay, a former football player, allege that "this case arises out of the NCAA and UNC's abject failure to safeguard and provide meaningful education to scholarship athletes who agree to attend UNC—and take the field—in exchange for academically sound instruction. This latest lapse, however profound, is regrettably just one of many such episodes in the history of college sports."[11] The incensed rhetoric of the complaint continues at the end of the opening section titled "Nature of the Action":

> This academic debacle, at one of the nation's finest public universities, could not have come as a surprise to the NCAA. . . . Instead, the NCAA sat idly by, permitting college sports programs to operate as diploma mills that compromise educational opportunities and the future job prospects of student-athletes for the sake of wins and revenues. . . . UNC's bogus classes once again reveal the great hypocrisy of college athletics in America. The NCAA and its member schools insist that their mission and purpose is to educate and to prevent the exploitation of college athletes. Yet it is the schools, the conferences, and the NCAA that are engaging in exploitation, subverting the educational mission in the service of the big business of college athletics—and then washing their hands of college athletes once they have served their purpose. (2, 3)

At the core of this lawsuit is an October 2014 report, which revealed some university employees directed roughly fifteen hundred student-athletes to sham classes. According to the report spearheaded by Kenneth Wainstein, a former official with the US Department of Justice, these cases of academic misconduct stretched over a twenty-year period, included 188 classes in the African and Afro-American studies department, and involved more than thirty-one hundred students—about half of which were student-athletes (Wainstein, Jay, and Kukowski 2014).

In the wake of the scandal, UNC's Chancellor, Carol Folt, fired or disciplined nine employees. One cannot draw a direct line of causality between sham classes, which inflate low GPAs to ensure athletic eligibility, and winning national championships. It takes more than strong GPAs to win a national championship; however, it is worth noting that during this twenty-year period, UNC athletics notched twenty national championships. One a year. Again, specific student-athletes or sports are not mentioned in this report, so it is unfair to accuse all sports at UNC from 1994 to 2014 of committing academic fraud. But, when an athletics program is found guilty of systematic cheating and academic fraud, a black cloud hangs over on all sports.

Though the NCAA was initially founded with the mission of protecting students' health, the NCAA has slowly morphed into passionately—and some would include *naively*—fighting to protect the amateurism and education of student-athletes. The NCAA has long repeated its mantra of "student first and athlete second." It also correctly argues that the majority of the one-half million student-athletes find professional careers outside their sports. Nevertheless, in its response to the lawsuit, the NCAA said it has no legal responsibility "to ensure the academic integrity of the courses offered to student-athletes at its member institutions" (quoted in Ganim, 2015; NCAA 2015). Donald Remy, NCAA chief legal officer, provided an additional view on the NCAA's response: "This case is troubling for a number of reasons, not the least of which is that the law does not and has never required the NCAA to ensure that every student-athlete is actually taking full advantage of the academic and athletic opportunities provided them" (quoted in Ganim, 2015).

Unfortunately, Remy and the NCAA are right here; McCants and Ramsay don't have a case. The governing of college sports is an overwhelming enterprise. Though I take issue with the NCAA over a number of its recent and historical decisions, I sympathize with an organization undertaking the Sisyphean task of monitoring over twelve hundred member institutions and the academic and physical well-being of close to one-half million student-athletes. Think about the other four major sports-governing bodies in the United States: the NFL includes thirty-two football teams; the MLB, NHL, and NBA each include thirty teams each. The NCAA not only oversees more teams and more players but also oversees more in general. The four major sports don't need to worry about protecting amateurism and making sure their players do not receive extra benefits. They don't have to worry about charting academics through a dizzying array of statistics, matrices, and initiatives. They just have worry about managing a profit and making sure their players stay out of handcuffs and make periodic public-service appearances.

Faced with the unenviable task of regulating almost all levels of collegiate sports, the NCAA, understandably, began delegating. This delegation allows voluntary institute members—remember, NCAA membership is voluntary—to set their own dictums for academic standards and enforcement. United States higher education embraces autonomy, and the NCAA has granted it through the NCAA Constitution, Article 2, Section 2.5, The Principle of Sound Academic Standards (National Collegiate Athletic Association 2017a): "Intercollegiate athletics programs shall be maintained as a vital component of the educational program, and student-athletes shall be an integral part of the student body. The admission, academic standing and academic progress of student-athletes shall be consistent with the policies and standards adopted by the institution for the student body in general." The NCAA does follow up Article 2, Section 2.5, in Section 16.3 "Academic Counseling/Support Services," but this section seems to repeat content previously covered in Section 2.5 and still leaves the issue of *how* up to individual schools:

> **16.3.1.1 Academic Counseling/Support Services.** Member institutions shall make general academic counseling and tutoring services available to all student-athletes. Such counseling and tutoring services may be provided by the department of athletics or the institution's nonathletics student support services. In addition, an institution, conference or the NCAA may finance other academic support, career counseling or personal development services that support the success of student-athletes.

Many high-profile and high-revenue Division I schools provide this academic support only through their athletics department, which may also include a wide variety of separate student-life services: career centers, dining halls, workout rooms, psychological and counseling centers, academic tutors and advisors, and writing centers. The Rankin M. Smith, Sr., Student-Athlete Academic Center at the University of Georgia, the Committed to an Athlete's Total Success program at the University of Arizona, and the Drew and Brittany Brees Student-Athlete Academic Center at Purdue, among others, direct resources to separate academic services for their highly valued student-athletes.

These separate academic services are the outcome of the multibillion-dollar industry of college sports growing alongside yet distinct from the general academic mission of US higher education. Moreover, these separate services seem more interested in protecting the big business that is college sports by ensuring student-athletes are always under the watch of the athletics department. Though there may be social and scholastic benefits to allocating resources to support only student-athletes, William Broussard (2004), who received a doctorate in rhetoric, composition, and the teaching of English from the University of Arizona and formerly the athletics department at Southern University, suggests this practice leads to "[student-athletes'] geographical . . . balkanization" (12). Such balkanization can be countered, Broussard holds, through "opening . . . channels of communication" between athletics departments and [writing program administrators] in hopes of "develop[ing] ways to help student-athletes develop critical consciousness . . . [and] pride in . . . their academic work" (12). I agree with Broussard, and in chapter 4, I illustrate the unfortunate outcome of student-athlete balkanization in regards to writing support but also the positive outcome of Broussard's suggestion of opening communication channels between (often) insular athletics departments and campus writing program administrators (WPAs).

Despite a history of faculty indifference, current insular athletics departments, and the many moments marking college sports' turbulent history, college sports and the many student-athletes are worthy of our attention. This is not to say composition studies scholars have not turned their attention to athletics. Debra Hawhee (2004), herself a former student-athlete, reminds us of the connections between early ancient Western rhetorics and athletics.[12] In *Bodily Arts: Rhetoric and Athletics in Ancient Greece*, Hawhee (2004) offers the "sophist-athlete" (65) as one who conceptually and *physically* refined rhetoric and rhetorical practices through public performances and contests. Julie Cheville (2001), in probably the most well-known text on student-athletes from within composition studies, spent two years studying the women's basketball team at the University of Iowa. Cheville's *Minding the Body: What Student Athletes Know about Learning* pulls from theories of embodied cognition, geography, situated cognition, and performance to illustrate the "conceptual disjunctures" (Cheville 2001, 8) between the classroom and the court in the hope that such an illustration "will encourage the integration of institutional structures and the revision of policies that have traditionally splintered athletic and academic programming in many institutions" (12). Though she does not use the term *transfer*, opting instead to think about "schematic portability" (Cheville 2001, 80) between learning contexts, issues of transfer animate her argument. She is concerned with "identifying the conceptual structures students face as they traverse multiple sites of learning within a single institution" (80). Cheville's prescient concern foreshadowed research coming about a decade later on how student-writers transfer knowledge and practice of writing across contexts, specifically the award-winning *Writing across Contexts:*

Transfer, Composition, and Sites of Writing by Kathleen Blake Yancey, Liane Robertson, and Kara Taczak (2014).

Continuing in the tradition of Hawhee and Cheville, I look to the (material) relationship between athletics and rhetoric. More specifically, I follow Cheville by turning attention to student-athletes competing within the NCAA. Like Cheville, I want to know our student-athletes and better understand the work we undertake with them. But I oscillate my focus differently than Cheville does. Cheville moves from broad to specific: her broad case of student-athletes' learning bounded spatially at a specific single institution. I move from specific to broad: the specific reading and writing practices of student-athletes across a wide range of NCAA member institutions. I want to get to know our student-athletes, not just our basketball players. And I believe our student-athletes are remarkably representative of our larger student population in ways we often do not consider. My implications do not just speak to athletic reform but to larger issues, namely how we can better work with our student-writers.

In *A Teaching Subject*, Joseph Harris (2012) famously describes composition—in all its iterations—as a teaching subject in that it "defines itself through an interest in the works students and teachers do together" (xv). The classroom is the heart of the work we undertake, the work we theorize, research, practice, and teach. Our discipline formed out of the classroom, no matter whether we locate this date back when Corax and Tisias were kicking around Sicily in the fifth century BCE or with the advent of FYC at Harvard in the late nineteenth century or with the founding of CCCC in 1949.[13] Unlike other disciplines, which moved from research to classroom practice, composition studies developed a research strand and its many journals and conferences from classroom practice. We are a student-centered discipline—so focused on our students that Kelly Ritter's (2013) chapter "Who Are Students?" opens Rita Malenczyk's (2013) edited collection *A Rhetoric for Writing Program Administrators*, a collection that positions itself as a primer for novice (and even experienced) WPAs. In *The Embodied Playbook: Writing Practices of Student-Athletes*, I focus on student-athletes as a subset of our student population.

The close to one-half million NCAA student-athletes know best through their bodies and use their bodies to engage with scripted plays. This engagement signals a unique form of literacy holding great promise for researchers invested in extracurricular forms of literacy and teachers invested in working with student-athlete writers. Over the past decade, I coached high-school soccer and basketball and worked with and in two prominent Division I athletics departments and one Division II athletics department. I supervised mandatory study hours for football players, developed curricula for a student-athlete writing center, hired and trained student-athlete writing tutors, and worked one on one with student-athletes who struggled mightily in the classroom and clung to eligibility. Through my many experiences across a range of institutions, I found myself constantly struck by the incongruity arising between the classroom and the court or field. I listened in on basketball film sessions and practices where coaches and players rapidly moved through complex sets of text. They teased apart slight bodily movement in a film clip, rewrote a play based on intuition, and collaboratively added a wrinkle to a play based on previous experience. I sat with a first-year football player who wrote out and explained the nuances of a wide-receiver route to me. These moments illustrate cognitive activities necessary to compete at a high level of sport, specifically metacognition and attention to audience, both of which inform textual revision. Aren't these cognitive activities necessary in a writing-intensive space?

Yet these student-athletes who unpacked their athletic knowledge and experience for me often struggled to slide words across the screen for their FYC assignments. I watched student-athletes struggle to connect how they know for their sport and how instructors ask them to know in a classroom. Without pointing an accusatory finger at the student-athletes, the NCAA, athletics departments, or even myself and my many colleagues who work with student-athlete writers, in this book I look hard at disconnects between the classroom and the court. I do this by listening to our student-athletes. When the NCAA and athletics departments periodically get serious about academic reform and implement a new conglomeration of matrices to track academic success (or failure), the voice of the student-athlete is often drowned in a cascading sea of press releases, data points, and Excel spreadsheets. Through giving voice to our student-athletes and their embodied writing practices, we can begin to get to know all of our students, not just those with traditional literacies.

THE BODY IN WRITING

In thinking about the writing practices of our student-athletes, I pair research from two growing areas: (1) work charting the constellation of extracurricular literate practices and activities students bring into the classroom and (2) work on the ineluctable relationship between the mind and body during cognitive activity. For the first, literacy researchers over the past two decades focus on charting instantiations of extracurricular literacy in a wide variety of locations and with a wide variety of artifacts. Theoretically, such work helps researchers arrive at new constructs of literacy and more robust theories for conceptualizing literacy and its place in school. Specifically, Kevin Roozen (2008) strengthens literacy researchers' understanding of activity theory and the interconnectedness of extracurricular and curricular composing through longitudinal ethnographic studies of writers. In his study of Charles, an African American undergraduate enrolled in a basic writing class and also a published writer, stand-up comedian, and spoken-word poet, Roozen focuses on Charles's opportunities to display publicly his literate development and how these opportunities informed his academic course work. Reading his original poems during the African American Cultural Center's weekly readings and performing jokes at his university's open mic night "enhanced [Charles's] speeches" (Roozen 2008, 24) for Speech Communication 101. Charles was failing the course midway through the semester, but in large part because of his extracurricular literacy work, he managed a passing grade. Roozen argues that "extracurricular and curricular literate activities . . . are so profoundly interconnected that it becomes difficult to see where one ends and others begin" (27). However, Roozen and other researchers investigating synergies and disconnects between school and nonschool literate practices miss two pieces to the literacy-development puzzle. I don't see much focus on how people take up literate practices as embodied literate practices or on the centrality of the body during meaning making practices. Both of these processes are central to how our student-athletes develop as writers, specifically, and literate persons, generally.

I find these missing pieces particularly curious when reading Mark Dressman, Sarah McCarthey, and Paul Prior's argument in their editor's introduction to an issue of *Research in the Teaching of English.* They assert, "Literate practices necessarily involve people's embodied acts and words" (Dressman, McCarthey, and Prior 2012, 5). We see this interdependent relationship between literate practices and the body in Roozen's (2008) exploration of Charles's literacy. Charles's involvement in stand-up comedy performances and public poetry recitations illuminated for Roozen how Charles's literate practices necessitated bodily interaction with text. Charles practiced how to "use written materials during an oral presentation, maintain[ing] eye contact with his audience, avoid[ing] using 'um' and 'uh,' and control[ing] his nerves" (22). Through honing these embodied literate practices, Charles passed Speech Comm, which, in turn, encouraged print-journalist aspirations.

Though I find myself nodding along with Roozen's narrative of and argument about Charles, what gives me pause is how Roozen casts Charles's engagement with embodied literate practices as subservient to his written (i.e., traditional) literate practices even though embodied practices appear central to his literate development. I am not diminishing the importance of written forms of literacy, but I am hesitant to place embodied forms of literacy, such as stand-up comedy and poetry recitations, as a steppingstone to more traditional engagements with literacy. Bodily engagement with text is an important piece of the larger puzzle of literate development.

The work of Jenn Fishman, Andrea Lunsford, Beth McGregor, and Mark Otuteye directly points toward the body's centrality during literate practices. Culling data from the Stanford Study of Writing, Fishman, Lunsford, McGregor, and Otuteye (2005) draw on curricular and extracurricular writing of 189 undergraduates at Stanford to report on synergies and disconnects between extracurricular writing—what the coauthors refer to as "live, scripted, and embodied activities . . . stage[d] outside the classroom" (226)—and the students' growth as academic writers. As is the case with Roozen's rich description of Charles, the coauthors' focus on embodiment is subservient to a focus on performance and how theories and practices of embodiment aid in the students' literate practices.

In the past two decades, we have seen work dedicated to constructing composition pedagogies grounded in bodily learning (see, for example, Barry Kroll's [2013] *The Open Hand: Arguing as the Art of Peace*). This work comes in the wake of the New London Group's nesting "bodily physicality" under "gestural design" (New London Group 1996, 83), and, only a few years later, Kristie Fleckenstein's (1999) succinctly and astutely asserting, "We are writing bodies" (297). However, many advances in understanding the body's role in cognition in general, let alone in writing, have come from outside composition studies. For one, philosopher Mark Johnson (1987) reminded us over three decades ago, "Our embodiment is essential to who we are" (13). Cognitive anthropologist Lambros Malafouris (2013) takes Johnson's statement further when he considers how the mind and body interact with material objects to undertake cognitive action. In *How Things Shape the Mind: A Theory of Material Engagement*, Malafouris seeks to "map a cognitive landscape in which brains, bodies, and things play equal roles in the drama of human cognitive becoming" (Malafouris 2013, 2). Advances in philosophy, computer science, and anthropology inform discussions within composition studies aimed at understanding the larger external and internal forces giving rise to the act of composing. I provide a more in-depth discussion of issues related to embodiment and writing in chapter 2 but here argue composition research should more clearly link literate practices, generally, and writing practices, specifically, with embodiment. We need to understand better how bodies intersect and interact with text during meaning making. In chapter 3, I illustrate how student-athletes know and become through bodily engagement with text. They understand the strengths and limitations of their rhetorical situation (to borrow rhetorical terms, they understand the *constraints*) through embodying the text and performing the text in a competitive space. As interest in extracurricular literate practices and embodied approaches to composing increases, we would do well to listen to our many student-athletes.

CHAPTER OVERVIEWS

Earlier in this chapter, I used a film metaphor to describe my focus in this book. Here I continue such a metaphor and offer my book in two sections sans an intermission. I title section 1 "Knowing Our Student-Athletes." Chapter 2 opens the curtain on this section, and I cast scripted plays as the lead performer. I look at how coaches and players construct plays, for whom plays are constructed, and to what end. Inspired by Charles Bazerman and Paul Prior's *What Writing Does and How It Does It* (Bazerman and Prior 2004), I ask what are plays and what do they do? To answer the first half of this query—what are plays?—I point to four contemporary basketball and football plays and one historical football play collected through digital and physical archival research. I define plays as multimodal texts, dialectically constructed, historically situated, and anticipative of competitive bodily enactment. In sum, plays respond to rhetorical situations affecting their composition. Often drawn by hand or digitally by coaches, plays reflect the offensive and defensive strengths of a team and represent a team's unification. For the second question—what do plays do?—I trace a play's creation and implementation. Using images of Auburn's and West Virginia's football team-signaling plays, I consider how plays as text interact with players. Early pioneers of football and basketball, such as Walter Camp at Chicago and James Naismith at Kansas, described clandestine methods for relaying plays to their players during a game. Following this tradition, the University of Oklahoma Sooners, and many other current football programs, use an amalgamation of images, gestures, and vocal cues to signal plays, and the basketball coaching staff at the University of North Georgia uses a similar combination of hand signals and vocal cues to relay a play quickly

and secretively during a game situation. Relayed plays undergo resemiotization, a term I borrow from semiotician Rick Iedema (2001; 2003). He
uses the term to describe the process by which meaning transfers across
various semiotic resources. After resemiotization, plays are embodied by
players. What do plays do? Plays, I contend, *do* competitive bodily action.
Understanding what plays are and what they do erects a stage for watching how student-athletes learn plays, as I do in chapter 3.

Chapters 3 and 4 provide concrete evidence for my claim regarding
the body's centrality during writing. Chapter 3 asks student-athletes to
take center stage. I report on a year-long case study into the men's basketball team at the University of North Georgia, a Division II school competing in the Peach Belt Conference with a roughly $3 million annual
budget. Through attending practices, sitting in on locker-room pre-
game, postgame, and halftime talks, interviewing players and coaches,
and collecting textual artifacts such as plays and scouting reports, I offer
a narrative of the 2014–2015 season and illustrate how coaches teach
plays and how players learn plays. Framing my argument with work on
material rhetorics by Laura Micciche (2014), locations of writing by
Nedra Reynolds (2004), and scaffolding by Isabelle Thompson (2009),
I argue players learn plays through three cognitive processes: spatial
orientation, haptic communication, and scaffolded situations. Like my
description of how players engage with plays, this three-step process is
predicated on knowing and learning through the body. Moreover, this
three-step process speaks to the larger question driving this book: how
do student-athletes know?

Chapter 4 opens the second section: "Teaching Our Student-
Athletes." In this chapter, I turn the spotlight to the material institutional context in which student-athletes write by offering an account
of a Division I athletics writing center at the University of Oklahoma
(OU), a prominent Division I school with nineteen varsity sports and
separate academic and student-life services for its student-athletes. For
four years, I worked as a program-development coordinator in this
space and experienced the material challenges of working with high-
profile student-athlete writers under the intense gaze of the athletics
department, the NCAA, and the public. Pulling from interviews with
athletics-department personnel—including the director of athletics—
and textual analysis of policy documents, I account for how stakeholders at various levels perceive and enact student-athlete writing tutoring.
Tutoring practices resulted from the NCAA's Section 2.5 found in the
NCAA manual for Division I Athletics. Fearful of violating this principle,
the athletics writing center handcuffed itself to unproductive methods

of working with student-athlete writers. Yet the center productively jettisoned these methods through forming intra-institutional alliances with campus WPAs, particularly WPAs at OU's campus-wide writing center. Compositionists and WPAs can use the collective capacity of those invested in writing to improve writing-related services for student-athletes while adhering to an NCAA academic principle. The act of teaching student-athlete writers, like teaching any writer, is caught in a matrix of material circumstances affecting how writing instruction may manifest itself. This chapter suggests methods for working with and against these material circumstances, which are unique for student-athlete writers. Once we better the conditions of teaching student-athletes, we can move into implementing pedagogies based on how they know. I do this in the final chapter.

My work with student-athletes at Auburn, Oklahoma, and the University of North Georgia culminates in chapter 5. I return to the three cognitive processes discussed in chapter 3 (spatial orientation, haptic communication, and scaffolded situations) that undergird the learning of scripted plays. I assert that the enactment of these plays, the embodied action of these plays, is analogous to another creative, collaborative activity reliant upon bodily reaction to an unfolding text: jazz improvisation. Recent work across fields such as business, ethnomusicology, and writing center studies has looked toward the learning practices of jazz improvisation as a model for other creative learning organizations. I specifically draw upon the work of Frank Barrett (1998), and of Elizabeth Boquet and Michele Eodice (2008), who extend Barrett's work to the writing center. I argue the learning of scripted plays looks a whole lot like the creative and collaborative model of learning extended from jazz to other learning organizations. Specifically, I argue for a pedagogy based on three of Barrett's characteristics of jazz improvisation:

- Shared orientation toward minimal structures that allow maximum flexibility;
- Distributed task: or continual negotiation and dialogue toward dynamic synchronization;
- Taking turns soloing and supporting (Barrett 1998, 606).

I return to the basketball players at UNG to show how these characteristics align with student-athletes' three cognitive processes for learning scripted plays. At the close, instead of provided specific pedagogical dictums based on these characteristics—doing so would counter the free-flowing spirit of jazz and sports—I give questions to consider when working with student-athlete writers. These questions capture the essence of a jazzy, creative, and collaborative learning, a way of learning founded on shared principles but manifesting its sonic and embodied experience in countless ways.

My argument throughout this book unfolds against the background of US higher education and its curiously cozy relationship with multibillion-dollar college sports. I aim to oxygenate nearly lifeless and impotent screeds directed at toppling the uniquely US phenomenon that is college sports by attending to how student-athletes produce and engage with text and providing curricular questions we can consider when working with this student population.

Finally, I am aware college sports, specifically, and the notion of scholarships for athletes, generally, are reserved for a select number of institutions across the United States. For example, Division III schools do not offer athletics scholarships. Many of my colleagues teach at schools without grant-in-aid scholarships for athletes or even an athletics department. Nevertheless, it's critical for college educators, particularly those of us teaching writing-intensive courses like FYC, to cultivate an awareness of how learners know through their bodies. I make this argument because recent advances in learning theories such as threshold concepts and the importance of writing transfer often rest on tapping into a learner's prior knowledge, not only curricular knowledge but also extracurricular, as Yancey, Robertson, and Taczak (2014) argue in *Writing across Contexts: Transfer, Composition, and Sites of Writing.* Our students' extracurricular prior knowledge is critical to the work we ask them to undertake in our classrooms, and understanding our student-athletes provides a foothold for understanding a much larger student population: those engaging with writing through their bodies. I suggest a large portion of *all* our students' extracurricular prior knowledge rests on a bodily literacy foundation. According to the Beginning College Survey of Student Engagement, 41 percent (n = 27,681) of students reported they were "very much" involved with "Athletic Teams" during their high-school years (Indiana University Bloomington Center for Postsecondary Research 2015). During the 2014–2015 school year, 7.8 million students competed in high-school sports, with over 2.1 million boys participating in football and/or basketball (the two most high-dollar athletic programs at the college level) (National Federation of High School Associations 2015). These high numbers continue into college even though a tiny percentage of students compete as student-athletes. In conjunction with the National Intramural-Recreational Sports Association, Scott Forrester (2014), a professor of recreation and leisure studies, surveyed over thirty-three thousand students. His data reveal 75 percent of students use on-campus recreation-center facilities or play intramurals, and 80 percent do so at least once a week. Only 21 percent never participate. Our students, not just our student-athletes, are physically active, though we often only see students' scholastic side. Students other than just student-athletes learn and make meaning through their bodies. These are the learners we need to consider—players of big-time college sports are just the ones grabbing the headlines. Through learning about our student-athletes, through learning how they understand text through their bodies, we learn about a great number of our students.

As we continue to chart our students' "funds of knowledge" (Moll and González 2001, 160) and understand how difference, manifested in myriad ways, impacts an individual's writing and entrance into curricular writing spaces, as we advocate on behalf of our students and those in our community, as we continue to explore how extracurricular instantiations of literacy impact curricular writing practices, we would do well to turn our gaze toward student-athletes and the athletic culture ingrained in many of our schools. When we open up new possibilities for what counts as literacy and how these new possibilities affect classroom practice, our eyes and ears should be sensitive to what our student-athletes are showing us and telling us. Let's stop thinking that what occurs on the athletic field does not affect the writing classroom. Let's consider the Treys and Jasons many of us teach and examine the writing practices of our student-athletes.

Notes

1. As I mentioned, college sports are a uniquely United States fixture. I remember sitting on a patio in Vernazza, Italy, with my wife. We were nibbling on octopus and talking with a group from New Zealand. Talk soon turned to sports, and the Kiwis drew a blank when I started on about college sports. The idea was completely foreign—literally and figuratively—to them.

2. Princeton, one of the oldest football programs in the nation, had a player-coach until 1901, the year prior to Woodrow Wilson's assuming the presidency of the school. One of the more humorous side notes regarding Princeton's football captaincy is that the captain in 1889 and 1890 was Edgar Allan Poe, grandnephew of the poet. Winthrop M. Daniels relays seeing then-professor Woodrow Wilson "come striding out upon the field, take his place behind the eleven with Captain Poe, and proceed to whip the team up and down the field" (Baker 1927, 14). Through this humorous anecdote, Daniels illustrates the seriousness with which the future university and US president approached football.

3. See John R. Thelin's (2004) *A History of American Higher Education* pages 159–60 for a more detailed account of the rise of mascots and pageantry in collegiate athletics.

4. Camp is an engaging figure. Often described as the "Father of American Football" (Smith 1990, 63), Camp wrote prolifically, penning articles for periodicals such as *Harper's Weekly*, as well as publishing a book of tactics for the card game bridge titled *Condensed Auction for the Busy Man*. Harford Powel's 1926 biography of Camp, while more of a panegyric of Camp than a critical examination of his life, examines how Camp helped usher football into being a major US sport governed by rules and overseen by the NCAA.

5. For additional reading on Stagg, see Robin Lester's (1999) *Stagg's University: The Rise, Decline, and Fall of Big-Time Football at Chicago*. Not only does Lester describe how Stagg consolidated power at an academically prestigious school, he also charts football's eventual abolishment at Chicago in 1939.

6. The student newspaper the *Wesleyan Argus* argued in 1888 that Wesleyan University should abandon football, but it appears the poor record of the team influenced the suggestion and not concerns over player safety or the possibility of athletics trespassing on academic turf. That year Woodrow Wilson, then a faculty member at Wesleyan, is said to have delivered an inspirational "blackboard talk" (Bragdon 1967, 172) before the Princeton-Wesleyan game, a game Wilson followed closely as a Princeton alum. During this talk, Wilson stressed "speed in running off plays" (Bragdon 1967, 172) over a century before a hurry-up style of offense would characterize the offensive attack of many college football teams. Unfortunately, Wesleyan would go on to lose to Princeton 44–0.

7. One reason for Eliot's losing the battle against football at Harvard was that he ran into then-president Theodore Roosevelt, a staunch proponent of the game. While Roosevelt admired the jingoistic tendencies of the game, he pushed hard for the game to be "played on a thoroughly clean basis" (Brands 1997, 553), especially after his son sustained an injury playing the game as an undergraduate at Harvard. When leading voices, including Eliot, pushed for abolishing the game because "its violence could not be curbed" (Dalton 2002, 290), Roosevelt invited representatives from Harvard, Yale, and Princeton to the White House in hopes of "minim[izing] the danger" without making the game "too ladylike" (Dalton 2002, 290). Walter Camp's biographer, Harford Powel, writes, "Nothing of great importance came from this meeting" (Powel 2008, 81); however, many historians point to this meeting as the first step toward the eventual formation of the Intercollegiate Athletic Association of the United States (later renamed the National Collegiate Athletic Association). For more information regarding Roosevelt's role in the formation of the NCAA, see John J. Miller's (2011) *The Big Scrum: How Teddy Roosevelt Saved Football*.

8. The financial numbers reported by Yale are a far cry from the record high $112.9 million reported in athletic expenditures at the University of Texas at Austin in 2009 (beating out the number-two school, The Ohio State University, by close to $10 million [Clotfelter 2011, 18]). These numbers speak to the dramatic growth of football and, since football often funds other college sports, college sports in general.

9. See Murray Sperber's (2000) *Beer and Circus: How Big-Time College Sports Is Crippling Undergraduate Education* and *College Sports, Inc.* (Sperber 1990); Mark Yost's (2010) *Varsity Green: A Behind the Scenes Look at Culture and Corruption in College Athletics*; Andrew Zimbalist's (1990) *Unpaid Professionals*; and Patricia Adler and Peter Adler's *Backboards and Blackboards: College Athletes and Role Engulfment* (Adler and Adler 1991).

10. Chicago reinstated its football program in 1973 but at the Division III level, at which student-athletes do not receive scholarships. Such a decision is a testament to Chicago's focus on academics over athletics.

11. Former football player Michael McAdoo also sued UNC over these fraudulent classes in November of 2014, just one month after Wainstein released the report. But

the lawsuit filed by Hausfeld LLP in Durham County (North Carolina) Superior Court on behalf of McCants and Ramsay is the first to point an accusatory finger at the NCAA.

12.   Hawhee played basketball at the University of Tennessee from 1988 to1992 under legendary coach Pat Summitt. The Lady Vols won two national championships during the four years Hawhee was on the team.

13.   Composition studies, or whichever discipline-encompassing term we use, is certainly a diverse and growing field. Following the lead of Edward M. White, Norbert Elliot, and Irvin Peckham (2015), my use of *our discipline* and *we* refers to the Classification of Instructional Programs 23.13 (Rhetoric and Composition/ Writing Studies; National Center for Education Statistics 2010). Within this specific classification is a host of program titles illustrating the capaciousness of our discipline: "writing, general; creative writing; professional, technical, business, and scientific writing, rhetoric and composition; rhetoric and composition/writing studies, other."

SECTION I

Knowing Our Student-Athletes

2

WHAT ARE PLAYS AND WHAT DO THEY DO?

A Textual Analysis of Football and Basketball Plays

[Early Yale football signals] were simple signals, but perhaps just as effective as the intricate mathematical symbols used nowadays, sometimes misunderstood in the moment of greatest need by a weary team.
—Harford Powel

Literate practices necessarily involve people's embodied acts and words
—Mark Dressman, Sarah McCarthey, and Paul Prior

Heading into the 2004 college football season, the Auburn Tigers were confident.[1] The previous season had taken the team and its fans on a rollercoaster ride of emotions complete with losing their first two games, watching the university president try unsuccessfully to fire the head coach, and beating rival Alabama and then Wisconsin in the Music City Bowl to end the season. The year 2004 looked promising. Auburn's offense was primed for a strong run. Jason Campbell returned at quarterback and Carnell Williams and Ronnie Brown at running back. In two years, all three would play in the NFL. Carlos Rogers and Jeremiah Ratcliff bolstered the defense. Both would also be drafted into the NFL after the season. On the shoulders of Rogers and Ratcliff, the Tigers' defense implemented plays such as Cov. 4 Play Action (see fig. 2.1), which relied on players to read the opposition and react accordingly. With this play and the student-athletes needed to embody this play, the Tigers sliced through their opponents, accumulating a 13–0 record, a Southeastern Conference (SEC) Championship, a Sugar Bowl victory, and a final number 2 ranking in the Associated Press and Coaches' Poll. Per game, the team yielded less than eleven points on defense and compiled an average margin of victory of over twenty points. The Associated Press named head coach Tommy Tubberville Coach of the Year. The

DOI: 10.7330/9781607326892.c002

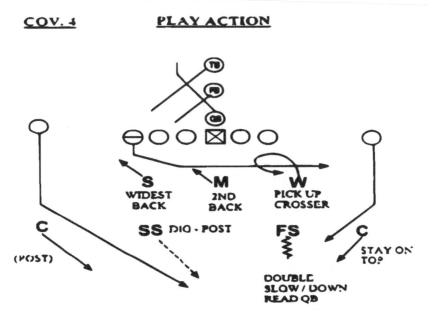

Figure 2.1. Auburn's 2004 defensive play Cov. 4 Play Action.

Tigers' success, like the success of any football or basketball team, was a result of individuals working in tandem with text.

My overarching query driving this book focuses on the writing practices of our student-athletes—how student-athletes engage with text for their sport. Before hearing from our student-athletes in chapter 3, I focus on the text our football and basketball players use. I ask, what physical texts are they engaging with and how? Using Stephen Witte's (1992) definition of text as "organized set of symbols or signs" (237), I look at plays coaches and players co-create and deliver through the player's body. In this chapter, I take a cue from Charles Bazerman and Paul Prior's (2004) *What Writing Does and How It Does It* and pose a seemingly simple query: what are plays and what do they do?

WHAT ARE PLAYS?

To answer the first half of this query—what are plays?—I draw from historical and contemporary plays I collected through digital and physical archival research. At the fore, I offer that scripted plays are multimodal texts, dialectically constructed, historically situated, and anticipative of competitive bodily enactment. Drawn by hand or digitally by coaches, plays reflect the offensive and defensive strengths of a team and represent a team's unification. Coaches collect plays into digital or physical playbooks, which they may disseminate to players to study on their own.[2] Auburn's play in figure 2.1 has three black holes on the left-hand side, indicating the utility of the text. It was three-hole punched for inclusion in a physical folder. During games, coaches prowl the sidelines with their playbooks tucked into the front of their pants, folded into a square in their back pocket, or written on an index card hidden in the inside pocket of a suit jacket. For some coaches, playbooks are more tome than book—upwards of four hundred plays individually labeled and systemically detailed. Other coaches take pride in representing their team's plays on a single index card. I have even talked with a coach who does not have a physical or digital copy of the team's plays. Though coaches compose and disseminate playbooks differently, all use plays to dictate movement during practice and a game.

When writing a play, coaches—like any writer—are responding to specific rhetorical situations. The audience (understood as the coach's own players and the opponents), exigence, purpose, constraints, and context faced by the coach-as-writer influence the invention, style, and delivery of the play, as well as how the coach and their coaching staff and players will memorize the play.

Auburn's Cov. 4 Play Action

Let's look at Auburn's defensive play in more detail.[3] First, a quick note on football terminology. Most teams divide the eleven defensive positions into three subsections: (1) defensive linemen, composed of defensive ends, defensive tackles, and/or a nose tackle; (2) linebackers, positioned behind the defensive linemen and composed of a middle linebacker, strong side, and weak side linebacker; and (3) defensive backs, positioned behind the linebackers, composed of cornerbacks and a free and/or strong safety. There are eleven players on the field, but Cov. 4 Play Action is directed to only the four defensive back (dbs)—hence the title *Cov. 4* where *Cov.* is short for *Cover*—and the three linebackers (lbs). To navigate around cumbersome position titles, players and coaches use abbreviations and nicknames: the middle linebacker is nicknamed Mike, the weak side linebacker is Will, and the strong side linebacker is Sam; these positions are further shortened to a single letter, as seen in the play. The dbs receive abbreviations: the cornerbacks are C, the strong safety is SS, and the free safety is FS.

While the lbs are trained to cover offensive players, the four dbs cover assigned zones of the field—four zones in a Cover 4 defensive scheme—and any offensive player who may enter that assigned zone. The phrase *play action* refers to the offensive play the defense predicts the offense will run. During a play action, the quarterback (QB) receives the ball and fakes a hand-off to the tailback (TB) with the halfback running ahead to block the defense. Ideally, the defense has been tricked by the fake hand-off and is rushing toward the TB, leaving the offensive receivers open to catch the ball. The QB, still in possession of the ball, runs to either side of the field to throw the ball to an open receiver.

To counter the play action, the defense needs to "read" the fake hand-off. Once they have successfully identified the fake hand-off, the defensive players cover the receivers. S covers the widest back. Here, the widest back would be the tailback. M is responsible for covering the 2nd back or the fullback. W is to pick up crosser. In this case, the crosser is the tight end. The dbs must stay in front of the receivers for this play to be effective. If a receiver's route leads into the middle of the field, then the SS covers him (i.e., dig post). The FS plays closer to the line of scrimmage and is responsible for reading the play action by the QB. Once the defense identifies play action, the FS drops back into coverage, waiting for a receiver to move into the center of the field.

As text, the chaotic sprinkling of squiggly and solid lines, Xs, squares, arrows, and numbers represents and communicates the reactionary play Cov. 4 Play Action. Moreover, the modes respond to specific rhetorical situations. When crafting plays, audience, purpose, exigence, constraints, and context are tied into invention, memory, and delivery. With a roster including four future first-round NFL draft picks, the coaching staff knew they had the players to run a Cover 4 defensive formation. The players— the *audience* in rhetorical terms—directly influenced this play. If Auburn found itself short on dbs or without a strong presence on the defensive line, a different play would have found its way into the playbook. The play's invention, drafting, and delivery directly hinged on who was on the field for the Tigers. The coaching staff also considered their opponents. Most of their opponents in the Southeastern Conference (SEC) had strong running games and looked to run first and pass second. The previous season, three of Auburn's conference opponents had running backs who eclipsed the one thousand-yard mark. These running backs collectively accumulated thirty-four rushing touchdowns. Conference-rival LSU shared the 2003 national championship with the University of Southern California, and five SEC teams finished in the top twenty-five. The AP and *USA Today* Coaches' Poll had five SEC teams in the top twenty-five of the 2004 preseason poll. Five of those teams included Georgia and LSU, both of whom were on Auburn's upcoming schedule.

Cov. 4 Play Action responded to the strengths of their opposition. Auburn coaches and players knew teams use a strong running game to set up a pass. Running the ball again and again and again causes the defense to creep closer to the line of scrimmage. With the defense expecting a run, the offense implements a play action by faking a run and throwing a long pass. The purpose, exigence, and context are wrapped into Auburn's awareness of its opponent's strengths and tendencies. The purpose and exigence, of course, is to negate a play action, a common offensive play within the run-heavy SEC conference context. And, finally, in hopes of ensuring that the players memorized the play, the coaching staff assigned a succinct name to the play (Cov. 4 Play Action) and provided an even briefer blurb detailing a player's assignment within the play (e.g., PICK UP CROSSER). The coaching staff ran the players through this play repeatedly in practice. Players memorized the play visually and then through their bodies, endlessly moving their bodies through the iterations of the unfolding play on the practice field in south Alabama. This play, and many others like it found in Auburn's thick defensive playbook, undergirded the Tigers' undefeated season, the third in the Tigers' 112-year history.

West Virginia's Reo 37

Seven hundred miles away, a different conference, and a different approach to the game—the mountains of Appalachia verses the plains of the Deep South. Yet both West Virginia and Auburn take great pride in their football teams and churn out high-level football players and plays. Since 2004, West Virginia and Auburn have had a combined sixty-six players drafted into the NFL and have notched nine conference championships and one national championship (Auburn in 2010). The play below comes from West Virginia's 2005 offensive playbook.[4] Like many playbooks, this one contains a thick introduction and an odd mix of pop psychology, thinly veiled biblical references, John Denver lyrics, and inspirational mantras. That season the team notched an 11–1 record—the lone loss dealt by Virginia Tech—and defeated Georgia in the Sugar Bowl. The Mountaineers won their second Big East championship, and then-head coach Rich Rodriguez received Big East Coach of the Year honors for the second time. The offense averaged over thirty-two points per game, exploding for over forty points three times. As Auburn's defense facilitated success, offense led to West Virigina's success.

Under Rodriguez, West Virginia used a zone read on offense, which works from the premise that it is easier for the offensive player to read

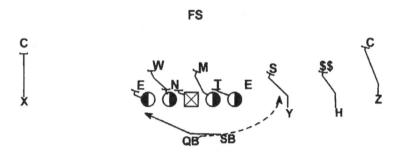

"REO 37"

Playside Assignment	Position	Backside Assignment
Zone palyside "A" gap - scoop. Ace You, Ace Tag – be alert for Triple	**Center**	
Zone playside "B" gap to LB vs. Odd or Odd Stack. Ace You vs. 1 technique. Ace Tag vs. strong shade	**Guard**	Slip or Scoop -- Cut off 1 Technique
Zone reach man on. Be alert for the over call (strong).	**Tackle**	Slip man on -- cut off block "B" gap cut off block to Hobo LB.
Open - cross over, stay on QB level until mesh, roll downhill to PST's butt.	**SB**	

X- Block Man Over		**H-** Block Man Over
Y- Block Man Over		**Z-** Block Man Over

QB- Secure the snap, eyes up, feet parallel and place the ball in the SB's belly. Bootleg opposite the play call past the L.O.S. holding DE.
Vs. Odd look, go under center, open at 5/7 o'clock with playside foot, seat ball and hand ball deep so SB can "bend". Bootleg opposite the play call past the L.O.S. holding DE.
* Possible sight adjustment vs. coverdown pressure.

Figure 2.2. West Virginia's Reo 37. The faded top-right corner was in the original.

a defender and run away from him than it is to block him. Once the quarterback receives the ball from the center, he reads the defense. If the quarterback sees the defense moving toward the ball, he does one thing; if he sees the defense remain still and wait for the play to develop, he does a different thing. In Reo 37, positions are referenced similarly to Auburn's play. After the center snaps the ball, the detailed alphabetic chart below the play instructs the wide receivers (X, Z, Y, and H) to run forward and trick their defenders into thinking a pass is coming. On the line of scrimmage, the two Es, the N, and the T positions have specific blocking assignments. The majority of the action capturing the attention of the fans in the stands and those in front of the television involves the quarterback (Q) and the running back (curiously titled SB, possibly for setback). The textbox directs Q to "secure the snap, eyes up, feet parallel and place the ball in the SB's belly." The QB then runs the opposite direction—hoping to distract the defense—and the SB runs around the right side of the line of scrimmage.

The premise behind the zone read sounds obvious enough—wait to see what the defense does and then act accordingly—but Rodriguez stumbled upon it by accident. Tim Layden's (2010) *Blood, Sweat and Chalk* traces important innovations in football plays. In his chapter on Rodriguez, Layden provides an account of Rodriguez's accidental discovery in 1990 at Glenville State College:

> One afternoon, Drenning [the quarterback] bobbled the snap on one of these zone-blocked running plays. Unable to get the handoff delivered to the running back, Drenning tucked the ball himself and saw the backside defensive end crashing down the line of scrimmage to tackle the running back—who . . . did not have the ball but was behaving as if he did . . . . [When a play is not run properly] the quarterback customarily follows the running back into the assigned hole and tries to salvage yardage. But Drenning, seeing the end closing, instead ran wide into the area vacated by the [defensive] end. . . . This . . . was the birth of the modern "zone-read." (165)

Once Rodriguez saw the play work in practice, he put it into a game. After coaching at Glenville State, Rodriguez landed a job as offensive coordinator at Tulane. Rodriguez brought the zone read with him. To enact the play, Rodriguez sought out athletic and quick quarterbacks—the audience for the play—who could read opposing defenses and run the ball when needed. Tulane went 12–0. Clemson hired Tulane's head coach, and Rodriguez made the move with him from Conference USA to the Atlantic Coast Conference. Again, Rodriguez succeeded, and he parlayed his success into the head-coaching gig at his alma mater: the University of West Virginia.

At West Virginia, Rodriguez recruited players capable of running his plays. Reo 37 and other zone-read offensive plays relied on an elusive and quick-thinking quarterback as the audience. In 2005, the date of the playbook from which Reo 37 is taken, Rodriguez brought in Pat White at quarterback. White was an athlete. He was Mr. Football for the state of Alabama and was drafted by Major League Baseball prior to signing with West Virginia. White ran the forty-yard dash—a standard length to measure a football player's speed—in an impressive 4.55 seconds.

At running back, the other critical audience for Reo 37, Rodriguez recruited Steve Slaton. Slaton was a short, powerful runner who also excelled at long jump. Combined, White and Slaton ended their freshman seasons with 2,995 total yards and twenty-four touchdowns. White was sixth in the nation with rushing yards per attempt, and Slaton was tied for seventh in the nation for touchdowns.

Michigan State's 54 Fist

Writing near the end of his life, the inventor of basketball, James Naismith (1941), mentioned people would often ask him what he believed to be the biggest change in basketball. He answered, "It is the skill of the players and the kind of plays that have been adopted" (63). Like football, basketball relies on an amalgamation of lines, shapes, and words to convey a basketball play. Played with five men, basketball is divided into positions that are, easily enough, numbered one through five. One is the point guard; two is the shooting guard; three is the small forward; four is the power forward; five is the center. Players are generally taller and heavier as the position numbers go up.

According to a 2015 *Forbes* report, the Michigan State men's basketball team is the tenth most valuable men's college basketball team. Valued at $17.1 million with a profit of just over $9 million, the Tom Izzo-coached team has notched eight Big Ten conference regular-season championships and twenty-one straight trips to the NCAA men's basketball tournament, winning it once in 2000 (Smith 2015). As a further testament to his coaching, Izzo helped six of his former assistant coaches land jobs coaching at Division I schools, and eighteen of his former players have been selected in the NBA draft. Plays are key to Izzo's lengthy success.

The play 54 Fist comes from the 2011–2012 basketball season. With then-president Barack Obama and a group of NBA Hall of Famers in attendance, Michigan State opened the season against North Carolina on the deck of the USS Carl Vinson, a ninety-five-thousand-ton Nimitz-class aircraft carrier off the coast of Coronado, California. Michigan State lost the game but went on to compile a 29–8 record, tying for first in the Big Ten and falling to Louisville in the Sweet Sixteen—the catchy term for the last remaining sixteen teams in the NCAA basketball tournament.

This scripted play asks the student-athlete playing the four position to score the basketball. As the focus is on five and four, the name of the play is *54 Fist*. When Izzo and his assistant coaches began constructing plays they would implement, they relied on the physical abilities—and even inabilities—of their players, just like the football coaching staff at

Michigan State
54 Fist

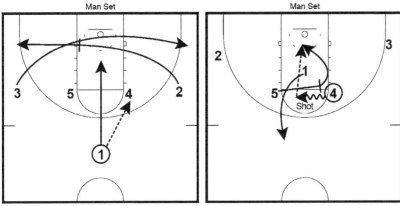

Man Set

- 2 sets a baseline screen for 3
- 1 enters the ball into 4 and cuts to the middle of the lane

- Once 1 gets into the lane, 5 comes across to set a ball screen for 4
- 1 flashes back to the key immediately after 5 starts getting into ball screen position
- 4 comes off of the ball screen for a pull up jumper or can hit 5 rolling to the rim

Figure 2.3. The play 54 Fist takes its name from the four and five positions responsible for the majority of the play's action.

Auburn and West Virginia. For 54 Fist to be effective against an opponent, Izzo needed a four who could handle, shoot, and pass the ball. As the four is one of taller and stronger players on the court, asking a four to do all these things is no easy task. During the 2011–2012 season, Izzo relied on senior Draymond Green. At Michigan State, Green was the third player in the history of the program to record a triple-double after he secured double digits in points, rebounds, and assists in one game. During the 2011–2012 season, Green, a team captain, averaged a double-double: over sixteen points and ten rebounds a game. The Golden State Warriors of the NBA drafted Green. With Green as a starter for the Warriors, the team won a championship in 2015, set the NBA record for wins in a season in 2016, and won the championship again in 2017. If one year Izzo finds himself with a four who struggles to handle, pass, and shoot the ball—who is more defensive minded than offensively talented—54 Fist may not make its way into the playbook. 54 Fist worked because of Green. As with football plays, the rhetorical situation surrounding the construction of a basketball play directly relies on the physical abilities of the players, who are the audience of the play.

Many of the modes present are also present in college football plays: the T shape representing screens, which are the basketball version of a block in football; zigzagged, dashed, or straight lines conveying movement; alphabetic text complementing the visual representation of the play. In 54 Fist, however, numbers instead of geometric shapes represent players, and the opposing team is missing from the play. Ball movement is broken into separate frames to show the progression of action. The player with the ball is circled. Dribbling is conveyed with a zigzag and a pass with a dashed line. Player movement without the ball is represented by a solid line.

This multimodal play has three layers of meaning through which readers sift. The iconic sign of the basketball court transposed as the play's backdrop forms the first.[5] Such a backdrop is critical for the invention and representation of a play and, as I will show in chapter 4, for student-athletes learning the play. Plays exist along a spatial grid—a *constraint*, to borrow a term from Keith Grant-Davie (1997) and Lloyd Bitzer. Though a basketball court is ninety-four feet long, the offensive action dictating this play is constrained to just one half of the court, a space forty-seven feet long and fifty feet wide. Within this space, the action is even more focused on the area inside the three-point arc, which is 20.75 feet from the basket. The three out-of-bounds lines within this offensive half and the half-court line—for teams cannot retreat back over the half-court line during a possession once they cross it—are further constraints through which bodily action is written onto the (discursive) space. And then there's the basketball goal itself. Bodily action swarms around this nexus. Bodily action would be aimless without the nexus. Even though grounding this play as text within the rhetorical constraints of the court is central for the construction of basketball plays, neither football play I examined offers such constrictive spatial grounding. Auburn, for one, is not concerned with where—in terms of distance (the fifty-, thirty-, twenty-yard line, for example) or side (left, right, or middle of the field)—the opposition will enact a play action. West Virginia is just as likely to run Reo 37 on its forty-yard line as on its opponent's forty-yard line. Certainly spatial constraints impact football plays (there are out-of-bounds lines; action is unidirectional and teleological; teams are more likely to run than pass the ball when one yard away from a touchdown), but the space is literally larger and does not seem to restrict action to the degree that basketball's tight twenty feet or so of action for ten bodies does.

Text inside the frame is the second layer of meaning for the reader to shift through; text outside the frame is the third layer. Like assembly instructions in which a picture of a physical action complements alphabetic text of that pictured action, these two layers of meaning in the Michigan State play convey the same information but use different modes to carry this information. The player's author makes use of lines, shapes, numbers, and alphabetic text inside the frame and makes use of only alphabetic text outside the frame. The verb *Shot* typed in the middle of the second frame is most curious. It is odd when alphabetic text designed to provide explanation for what occurs inside the frame invades the frame. It is as if the author did not trust any mode—not an image, a line, a shape—other than alphabetic text to convey the most important message of this play: when and where to shoot the ball. In this play, lines represent movement, numbers represent players, and circles represent who has the ball. However, these modes are not capable, the play's author suggests, of representing when and where to shoot the ball. Within discussions of multimodality, alphabetic text is often jettisoned in favor of or placed as concomitant with other modes of meaning making. With 54 Fist, complementary function between alphabetic text and other modes is lost. Alphabetic text reigns supreme.

Arizona State University's Nike

West Virginia, Auburn, and Michigan State achieved recent high-level success on the athletic field for the respective sports from which these plays came.[6] Auburn and Michigan State have even won national championships since 2000. West Virginia would have played for a national championship in 2007 but lost to rival Pittsburgh in the last game of the regular season. But not so with Arizona State. A solid but not excellent athletics program, Arizona State has flirted with high-level success yet has never made a habit of being at the top of the Pac-12 conference or national standings in basketball or football.

Arizona State's basketball had a program-high Elite Eight appearance in the NCAA tournament in 1985 but has only been to the NCAA tournament twice under Herb Sendek, who led the team from 2006 to 2015. Under current coach, Bobby Hurley, the team made the tournament in 2018. I bring this up and juxtapose Arizona State's struggles in basketball with Michigan State's successes to show that in either case—a solid or struggling program—coaches construct plays in the same manner. No matter whether we are looking at Duke, one of the top teams in the nation, or at a tiny Division III college struggling to suit five players to field a team, college basketball coaches are constructing and implementing multimodal plays.

Nike

Arizona State

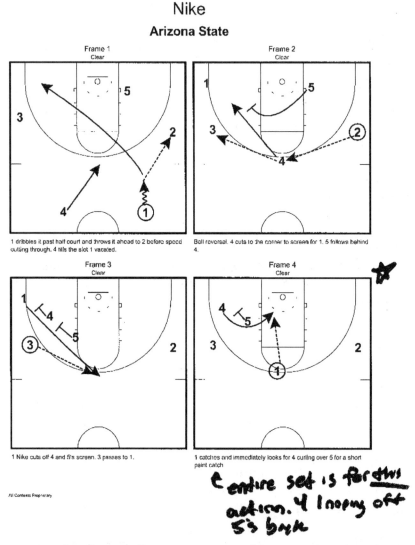

Figure 2.4. Through its use of lines to represent spatial direction and morphing players into symbols, Arizona State's Nike draws parallels to the multimodal football plays examined earlier.

The symbolic and iconic symbols, the multiple modes, the layering of meaning, and the use of framing are all seen in Nike. Here a wrinkle arises: metacognitive writing. After the play was transcribed and printed onto sheets of paper, either the head coach or an assistant coach marked on top of the play. This marking added a fourth layer of meaning. Unlike the inclusion of the word *Shot* in 54 Fist, this alphabetic text exists outside the frame and seems to act as an addendum to the alphabetic text under frame four. I am not sure why the coach added this note. Maybe his players did not understand the play or maybe he forgot to add this detail earlier before transcribing the play. This addendum reveals that multimodal texts in this community of practice are not closed and finalized texts. Texts are always under construction, always being revised. Plays are a working dialogue between players and coaches, between coaches, and even between players. In this sense, they are dialectically constructed, evidence of a collaborative relationship between coach and player.

Oklahoma's 1942 Football Play

Plays such as Reo 37 and Nike operate in a rich and lengthy history of incorporating multiple modes to convey meaning. The Western History Collections at the University of Oklahoma houses a 1942 football playbook used by then-head coach Dewey William "Snorter" Luster. Luster coached the Oklahoma Sooner football team in the midforties. He faced challenges fielding a full team with World War II raging, but he continued OU's strong football tradition by winning two conference championships during his five years in charge. I first came across one of Luster's plays (see fig. 2.5) in a display case inside Oklahoma's athletics department, where I worked for four years. The Western History Collections loaned similar items to the athletics department: a football program from the early days, buttons, pennants, images, and hand-drawn football plays, which grabbed my attention as I made my daily walk to my cubicle. The display cases were in a highly trafficked area, yet I found their placement odd. The only feet walking past the cases were those connected with the athletics department: faculty, staff, or student-athletes. The general student body did not travel this space, and the community was not allowed. As such, the display cases stood as an homage to, well, themselves, to us in the athletics department. Most displays of this sort are present to teach those outside a culture about a culture. Instead, here on the third floor of the football stadium, our caged curios stood for our past, representing a culture to a culture.

One day they were gone, replaced by large framed posters of bowl games from days past. I made a trip over to the Western History Collections to browse through the documents once on display. The student working the desk that day handed me the entire bound playbook from which this play was taken. I carefully flipped through the delicate pages onto which Luster wrote his plays. He diagrammed all plays in colored

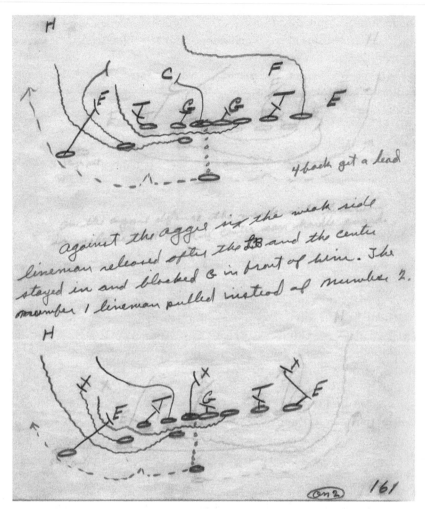

Figure 2.5. The top and bottom plays are similar except for some slight variation in the blocking scheme on the far right side on both plays. The cursive text, composed in past tense, reads, "Against the Aggie [the former nickname of Oklahoma State] six the weak side lineman reloaded after the LB [linebacker] and the center stayed in and blocked G [a guard] in front of him. The number 1 lineman pulled instead of number 2." The original play is in colored pencil: the defensive positions in black, the blocking schemes in blue, and the dashed line shooting off to the left, in red. (Courtesy of the Dewey "Snorter" Luster Collection, Box 4, Item 1, Western History Collections, University of Oklahoma Libraries.)

pencil with occasional pen markings. Unlike the Auburn and West Virginia playbooks, which I too examined in their entirety, this one did not appear to have been bound in any discernible order. Contemporary playbooks usually start with team mantras, inspirational quotes, an overview of the goals for the season, and basic formations through which the majority of plays will be run. And then the diagrammed plays begin. Luster's playbook was strictly plays, as if the audience for the text was Luster and not his coaching staff, his players. Contemporary playbooks are meant for the larger team audience. Luster's was inward focused. Some of the plays have sentences scrawled across them, which Luster constructed in the past tense as if remembering what worked against the opponent.

Fast forward seventy years and contemporary football plays are quite similar. Coaches still use geometric shapes, abbreviations, and lines as representational modes. Circles represent the offensive players; E, T, and G represent the ends, the tackles, and the guards. Long T-shaped lines still represent blocks. A dashed line with an optimistic arrow pointing toward the end zone still represents an individual running the ball downfield. Although Luster constructed his play for football and not basketball, it shares commonalities with the Arizona State play because both include important marginalia. These marginalia led to the *doing* aspect of the play as text: the result of the play being bodily enacted during practice or a game by a player.

This brief overview of historical and contemporary, hand-drawn and digitally drawn, plays offers plays as multimodal text, dialectically constructed, historically situated, and anticipative of competitive bodily enactment. Plays are textual evidence of a working dialogue between coaches and players. This dialogue may take on the guise of spoken dialogue. In chapter 3, I describe my year-long research into a Division II men's basketball team. During the first practice I attended, the head coach stopped his players when they were running a play. The players stood with hands on hips, sweat beading on foreheads, while the head coach orally adjusted the play. One of the seniors on the team spoke up and suggested a similar adjustment to a different play. The head coach agreed and made the change aloud. The collective team dialectically constructed plays based on the shared needs of the audience (the players) and the authors (the coaches). Here, the line between audience and author is blurred, and player/coach coauthorship results in a play. Yet even if an actual dialogue does not begin between players and coaches, like the one I witnessed, coaches as authors construct plays with an awareness of their players' physical capabilities. At Michigan State, Izzo needs an offensively minded small forward in the four position; Auburn needs smart dbs for its play action; Rodriguez needs an adroit and speedy quarterback for his zone read. Plays are dialectically constructed. Moreover, plays as text draw from a rich repository of historical modes of meaning making. As the 1942 Oklahoma play illustrates, plays contain common and historically sedimented modes. Coaches draw upon this tradition when diagramming plays as texts. A T-shaped line has long represented a block on the football field and a screen on the basketball court; arrows have long indicated directional movement; players have long been represented via shapes and positions with abbreviated alphabetic text and symbols. Critical information has long been represented in alphabetic text: the *Shot* in Michigan State's play, the metacognitive marginalia in Luster's play. Football and basketball change in other ways (e.g., more football teams pass today than in 1942; college basketball implemented the three-point shot). However, the modes used to represent meaning have largely held firm. Play authorship draws on histories of meaning making. Yet most important, plays anticipate competitive bodily enactment. Accolades are not awarded for plays. A team wins a game and accolades are showered on players, coaches, and programs based on the effective *embodiment* of these plays. Plays are created, or not, based on the physical and embodied capability of players. The body is the driving rhetorical force behind the creation of a text. Text is created for the body. Asking how plays are embodied leads into the second part of my framing query: what do plays do?

WHAT DO THEY DO?

In turning to the second part of my framing query—what do they do?—I consider how plays as text interact with players. To state my argument at the fore, coaches, players, and opponents cause plays to undergo resemiotization, a term describing the process of meaning transferring across semiotic resources. Plays begin as physical text, as in the play in figure 2.2. Yet such text is bulky and not easily transmitted to players. Through signals—sometimes oral, sometimes visual, sometimes gestural—teams devise unique ways to transmit their plays rapidly and secretively during a game.

Once plays undergo resemiotization, plays are embodied by players. In brief, plays *do* competitive bodily action. With the term *resemiotization* I draw on the work of self-described "socio-semiotic ethnographer" Rick Iedema (2001; 2003). Iedema explains that resemiotization is "about how meaning-making shifts from context to context, from practice to practice, or from one stage of a practice to the next" (Iedema 2003, 41). As a concrete example, Iedema points to his study of the first meeting of a mental hospital planning project. Health officials, architects, engineers, and future users of the building were present at the meeting.

Following five meetings, hours of recorded talk, numerous drafts of a report, and several two-dimensional drawings, all in attendance signed off on the building plan, and construction began. In this example, meaning is shifted linearly across semiotic resources—talk, alphabetic text, drawing. In an additional example provided by Bruno Latour (2006) and explored by Iedema, a person reminds another person to close the door; a sign stating such is taped to the door; a hydraulic door-closing device is installed. Like Iedema's example of the planning project moving from one semiotic resource to another, Latour illustrates how everyday practices follow similar steps. But what holds Iedema's attention and what makes resemiotization such a curious phenomenon worthy of our attention is "how this [planning] project moves from temporal kinds of meaning making, such as talk and gesture, towards increasingly durable kinds of meaning making, such as printed reports, designs, and, ultimately, buildings" (Iedema 2001, 23, 24). In other words, a resemiotization trajectory focuses attention on how meaning is leveraged across semiotic resources of increasingly "durable manifestations." For Latour, durable manifestation occurs when meaning moves from talking about installing a door-closing device to actually installing a door-closing device.

Tracing a resemiotization trajectory is important for two reasons. One, Iedema argues that meaning shifts across semiotic resources because of the constraints and affordances of these resources (Iedema 2001, 33). Thus a shift from, say, a scripted football play to a gestured football play signals a shift in the needs of the audience and/or rhetor. Two, Iedema suggests the entire planning project he studied "weave[s] people and their meaning into increasingly reified, complex, and obdurate semiotics" (Iedema 2001, 35), particularly because resemiotization stresses "*social construction*" (Iedema 2003, 50; emphasis in original) over textual representation. Thus, resemiotization describes "socially recognizable and practically meaningful artifacts" (50). Here, one can think of a football or basketball play: a text recognizable to members of that community of practice and undertaking the practical function of coordinating bodily movement. Attention to such social construction invites an analysis of the modes used in the construction of a text, why specific semiotic resources were leveraged, and what these rhetorical decisions say about the audience and the rhetor.

In his biography of Walter Camp, long considered the progenitor of US football, Harford Powel (2008) offers insight into Camp's early innovations to the game. Not only did Camp invent the quarterback position, the line of scrimmage, the safety, and the set of downs, he is also credited as the first to use signals to send plays. Describing Camp's time as Yale head football coach from 1888 to 1892, Powel writes,

> The use of signals to inform the team what play was to be used—without at the same time informing the adversaries—was also a logical development which Walter Camp was first to recognize and first to use. The code of signals given to Yale was ludicrously simple, providing for only four plays. The signals were not numerals, as at present [1970], but short sentences. Each entire sentence indicated a play, the omission of one word, and then another, serving to hide the meaning. . . . And the sentence, "Play up sharp, Charley," or any part of it, would indicate that the ball would be passed through quarterback to [player] W. Terry for a run to the left. These were simple signals, but perhaps just as effective as the intricate mathematical symbols used nowadays, sometimes misunderstood in the moment of greatest need by a weary team. (56, 57)

Amos Alonzo Stagg played under Camp at Yale and then went on to a Hall of Fame coaching career at the University of Chicago. Stagg expresses similar remembrances of early football signals: "Yale's 1888 signals were given entirely by the position of the captain's hands. [Team captain William] Corbin graduated in 1889, and that fall we began with a system of key words and phrases, switching to numbers late in the season" (Stagg and Stout 1927, 126). Stagg provides a sampling of phrases used by Yale. He writes that if the quarterback were to "speak to the right rusher," then the running back would run the ball to the "left half around the end." He continues with a listing of other verbal cues:

- Praising any play—left half between right tackle and end.
- Condemning any play—right half between left tackle and end.
- Speak of any part of the torso—left half between left guard and center.
- Anything with vim or life—left half between right guard and tackle.
- Anything denoting lifelessness—right half between left guard and tackle (126).

Current teams cloak their signals in increasing levels of secrecy with a dizzying combination of image, gesture, and alphabetic text. But Camp and Stagg cautioned against such complexity. Stagg writes, "[Signals] became more and more complex in the later [18]90's, running into problems in addition, multiplications, subtraction, even division, until football threatened to become an advanced course in mental arithmetic. Long signal drills were held at night. Such complexity defeated itself and more ground was lost by the inability of players to remember their own signals than was gained through the opposition's mystification" (Stagg and Stout 1927, 127).

In these football examples, the meaning inherent in a play as text is transferred into a different semiotic resource, that of talk, in response to rhetorical demands. Powel (2008, 56) describes the process of using signals without informing the "adversaries" as a "logical development." Camp kept the code of signals simple with easily memorized sentences. Like Camp, Stagg used pithy sentences to signal plays. The exact sentences uttered appeared to be at the discretion of the signal caller. As long as the sentence spoke of any part of the torso, for example, the team would prepare to run the ball on the left half between the left guard and center. At this point in the development of football, the process of resemiotization is linear and three step: from a handwritten play, to sentence, to bodily action. Here we see how plays as text cycle through various communicative modes in response to the larger rhetorical situation in which they are enacted. Yet the plays were also cyclical. A poorly or perfectly executed bodily action would influence the choice of the next handwritten play for the team to implement.

I propose resemiotization as a useful tool for focusing attention on what plays do. Resemiotization allows writing researchers to uncover how student-athletes leverage different reading and writing practices when engaging with text. More important, it allows compositionists to see how these practices "locate . . . writing and composing in situ over time in longer chains of distributed activity" (Gilje 2010, 497). With this phrase "distributed activity," Øystein Gilje (2010) calls to mind the work of Paul Prior (1998) and other writers such as Jody Shipka (2011), Kevin Roozen (2008; 2009), and Edwin Hutchins (1995) interested in cognitive tasks like writing and how writing is a single link in a chain of meaning making activities used by a community sharing a "single historical trajectory" (Gilje 2010, 497). Such an understanding of literate activity resonates with college sports.

Resemiotization and a Play

Scripted plays are resemiotized across various modes and states of semiotic resources: alphabetic text, placards, hand signals, verbal cues. Though Iedema (2001) considers how resemiotization moves from "temporal kinds of meaning-making . . . towards increasingly durable kinds" (23, 24), football and basketball take a cyclical approach. Let's get concrete by returning to Auburn's play Cov. 4 Play Action, the first scripted play offered in this chapter.

Auburn's coaches assign plays succinct names and then translate plays into numbers. These numbers are painted onto large yellow cardboard

Figure 2.6. Signaling the defensive play, a coach holds up a yellow sign inscribed with a black number. Notice the thick stack of cards in his left hand. Unfortunately, the picture is not able to capture the quick gesticulations of the two coaches on either side. (Photograph taken by the author).

squares and translated into hand signals. In a game situation, three coaches flash signs to the defense before a play. Two coaches use hand signals and one coach holds up a yellow card. Two of the coaches send "dummy" signals. Figure 2.6 comes from a November 2008 match-up between Auburn and Georgia. My wife and I arrived at a game close to two hours before kickoff to get seats close to the sidelines so I could snap pictures of the coaches relaying plays (I might have been the only one arriving early for such a purpose). We sat a few rows behind the end zone, and I spent the majority of the time not watching the Tigers take on the Bulldogs but on how the defensive coaches signaled plays. The static image does not offer the quick gesticulations made by the two other coaches; however, the yellow card is seen in the middle of the photo.

Once a student-athlete learns a play, be it through sofa cushions as detailed in chapter 1 or via a more traditional route, plays follow a rapid, linear, and predetermined path during a game or practice as teams only have forty seconds to receive and prepare to run a new play. Immediately after the refs whistle the previous play to a stop, a coach (sometimes the head coach) speaks through his headset to an assistant coach, graduate assistant, or backup quarterback. The recipient of the message transfers the verbal play into hand signals or flashes placards with textual inscriptions. The captains on the field see the hand signals or placard and transfer the visual representation of the play into a verbal representation, which they shout to their teammates. Mike—the middle linebacker—and the strong safety are in charge of changing the play and/or ensuring their particular section of the defense receives the correct play. At this point, the scripted play is not an empty document. It becomes embodied and enacted on the field.

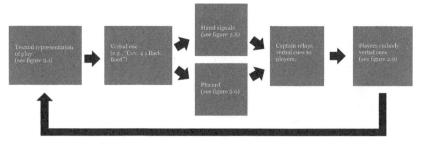

Figure 2.7. A graphic representation of a play's movement.

If the offense does not change its formation once the players have broken the huddle, the defense runs the play as scripted. If there is any variety of offensive formation, it is up to Mike and the strong safety to react properly and adapt the play. A defensive alignment, however, is not solely a reaction to the offensive formation. Down count, distance to the goal line, time left on the game clock, and various constituencies of the rhetorical situation influence the decision regarding when and where to embody a particular play. Once the center snaps the ball to the quarterback, a play lasts an average of three to five seconds. When these few seconds have elapsed, a new play is relayed to the defense and the cycle begins anew. A coach selects a play and orally delivers it to another set of coaches or players on the sidelines, who translate the play into gestural or visual cues, and captains relay the play on to their teammates on the field. The center snaps the ball; the play lasts five or so seconds; the cycle continues.

David Biderman (January 15, 2010) reports in the *Wall Street Journal* that an NFL game broadcast on a major network has an average of eleven minutes of action. NFL games, like college football games, are sixty minutes long. Yet, football is the only major sport in the United States in which the clocks run even though the players may not be playing. Thus, forty-nine minutes of an NFL game are devoted to coaches and players moving text. Though we are not concerned with the NFL, such results speak to the large corpus of text trafficked through a high-level football game. Even though coaches and players take great pains to push text across multiple semiotic resources and multiple audiences and senders rapidly, forty-nine minutes are devoted to text distribution and comprehension. Only a small portion is devoted to embodying the text.

Like Auburn, West Virginia uses dummy hand signals and large placards with numbers or letters. Figure 2.8 is taken from a 2013 matchup between Oklahoma and West Virginia, which Oklahoma won 16–7.

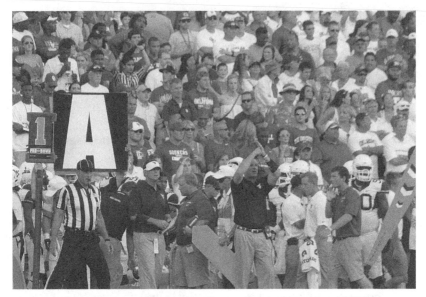

Figure 2.8. West Virginia coaches signaling plays against the University of Oklahoma. (Photo by Valorie Wakefield. Used with permission.)

The down (first down) and large sea of opposing fans in red are visible. One coach, with hands raised in a slanted T shape, sends gestural signs; another coach, blocked in the picture by the ref, holds a large placard with an *A* on it over his head. As with Auburn's signals, one of these coaches may be sending a dummy signal, or these two signs may be complementary. Because of the relatively slow overall pace of football—remember, little of the game is devoted to playing the game and a sixty-minute college game lasts an average of three hours and twenty-three minutes (Solomon 2015)—and the need for greater secrecy in play calling, football coaches generate more complex signals to relay their plays as text.

Basketball is different. When I worked closely with the men's basketball team at the University of North Georgia, work informing chapter 3, I talked with the head coach, Chris Faulkner, about play calling and hand signals. Football coaches dictate all offensive and defensive plays during a game. Basketball coaches often allow their players, generally the point guards, to dictate the plays and flow of the game. Faulkner does signal plays following time-outs, during in-bounds plays, and when he feels the team needs a different focus, and he uses verbal and gestural cues to signal plays. Faulkner's team has a series of offensive plays called *Up series.* Within this series, the team has different plays corresponding with different parts of the body: ear, chin, elbow. From the sideline, Faulkner will shout "Up ear" and tug on his lobe, yell "Up elbow" and pat his elbow. He sends the signal to the whole team and relies on the point guard to ensure all players on the court hear the call. If Faulkner is not signaling the play, the point guard is responsible for verbally calling a play and adding the gestural cue. I have yet to see a basketball team—at any level—use placards or have multiple people on the sidelines send potential dummy signals in hopes of tricking the opposition. Partly, this is due to how players learn plays, which I detail in the next chapter, and the emphasis coaches place on players learning how to improvise within a tightly structured play. Faulkner teaches his players to improvise within a play and not follow the play exactly as it is scripted. This concept of improvisation is critical to how student-athletes know and engage with text, holding great promise for how we might work with student-athletes in the writing classroom, which I detail later in this book. For now, I'll end by mentioning that if the play breaks down for any number of reasons, the players are able to improvise during the unfolding of the play. Football does offer glimpses into players improvising within a tightly scripted play, but football is much more tightly scripted and controlled by the authors of the plays, the coaches.

Iedema (2001) states resemiotization drives toward "more durable materialities" (26). Football and basketball plays expand this notion by allowing users to shift back and forth between temporal and durable semiotic resources depending on the rhetorical context. A play may begin in a durable medium—sketched on a sheet of paper—and then move toward a less durable medium—talk—and then back to a placard and then to a vocal cue. A play's discursive and recursive trajectory does not follow the linear path laid out by Iedema. Plays follow a messy trajectory hinging on the constraints and affordances of the mode used by the players and coaches and the embodied capabilities of the players. The end goal of cyclical, secretive resemiotization for football and basketball is to either score points or stop a team from scoring points. For that to happen, the play must be embodied by the players on the field.

The Embodiment of Plays

What do plays do? Once resemiotized, plays display embodied action. During practice or a game, a student-athlete's embodiment of a play reflects how they understand the play. In public, a player properly or poorly embodies this text, and the people in the stands and watching on television bear witness to this attempt. Effective understanding of a play is effective embodiment. Highlighting the role of the body within this community of practice is crucial. In *The Body in the Mind*, philosopher

Mark Johnson (1987) writes, "Our embodiment is essential to who we are, to what meaning is, and to our ability to draw rational inferences and be creative" (13). Johnson attributes creativity and rationality to an embodied sense of our self. Through the phrase "what meaning is," Johnson tiptoes close to discussions linking embodiment with epistemology, even more intriguing to composition studies because epistemology, according to James Berlin (1988) and others, undergirds theories of composition. Kristie Fleckenstein's (1999) argument dovetails with Berlin's interest in epistemology and Johnson's work with embodiment. Fleckenstein holds that "we write as bodies. . . . We immerse ourselves in . . . our own bodily reactions as writers. We *are* our bodies; we are writing bodies" (Fleckenstein 1999, 297; emphasis in original). Like Fleckenstein, Margaret Syverson (1999) contends that our understanding of writing and subsequent pedagogy of writing should account for the central role the body plays in composing since "writers, readers, and texts have physical bodies and consequently not only the content but the process of their interaction is dependent on, and reflective of, physical experience" (12). Syverson's inclusion of "texts" in the listing of things that have a physical body stands out to me. Syverson moves past the myopic view of the embodiment of animate objects and suggests exploring how the physical existence and attributes of the text before us—be it a book, a scrap of paper, a PDF—facilitates or stymies its attempt to carry meaning. Though this point may be clear enough, Syverson holds that "one of the salient features of academic life is the massive suppression of awareness of this physical relationship" (12), namely our tactile interaction with text.

Recent scholarship within composition studies takes up Syverson's work and examines intersections of the body and composing. A. Abby Knoblauch (2012) classifies what she terms "embodied terminology" (50). Delineating embodied terminology into three terms ("embodied language," "embodied knowledge," and "embodied rhetoric"), Knoblauch attempts to "differentiate the ways in which we talk about embodiment, particularly within English studies broadly, and Composition and Rhetoric more specifically" (51). Doing so and not erroneously conflating the terms (as Knoblauch believes previous scholarship has done) allows "embodied writing and ways of knowing within the academy" (51) to no longer be marginalized. Defining embodied knowledge as "that sense of knowing something *through* the body" (52; emphasis in original), Knoblauch provides a succinct definition of embodied rhetoric: a "purposeful decision to include embodied knowledge and social positionalities as forms of meaning making within a text itself" (52). Such a definition connects strongly with the forms of embodiment seen in college football, which I detail shortly. Moreover, it calls to mind Kathryn Perry's (2012) powerful query in her *Kairos* webtext on dance and composing: "How do we distinguish between the physical and conceptual work of composing?" This question strikes to the heart of the warrant undergirding Fleckenstein's claim that "we are writing bodies," and the efficacy of Fleckenstein's claim casts Perry's query as all the more pertinent. Perry leaves her audience to ponder this question, leaving blurred the delineation between physical and conceptual, the body and the mind. This blurring is especially evident in how student-athletes approach plays as forms of multimodal embodied texts.

Connecting more directly with multimodality, Gunther Kress (2010) underscores the centrality of the body when he argues that interest in multimodality "represents a move away from high abstraction to the specific, the material; from the mentalistic to the *bodily*" (13; emphasis added). Kress carves space for a rich discussion of embodiment with the use of "bodily." However, he fails to fill this space and largely restricts his theory on multimodality to texts. He does not investigate how the body interacts with and through these texts. In thinking about college football plays as doing bodily action, attention to embodiment highlights the inclusion of a vital mode used during the composing process: skin and bones, beating heart and breathing lungs—the physical body. Theories of embodiment help us capture how, in the words of Dressman, McCarthey, and Prior (2012), "literate practices necessarily involve people's embodied acts and words" (5). This quote is an epigraph to this chapter and is critical to how I approach this book. Found in their editors' introduction to *Research in the Teaching of English*, Dressman, McCarthey, and Prior asks us to consider how theories of embodiment capture the inextricable link of the body and mind during composing, how our skin and bones impact our writing, how our breathing and heartbeat impact how and what we write.

Despite all the work constructing and teaching a play and then transferring it across various semiotic resources, the play remains an empty vessel—a multimodal text such as in figure 2.1, a letter as in figure 2.8, or hand signal as in figure 2.8—until it is embodied on the field (see fig. 2.9). When coaches and players visually flash a play to the captains, and when the captains verbally relay the play to their teammates, the play ceases to be a floating and empty text. It becomes anchored by the body to concrete action. Prior to public embodiment, plays are clandestine documents, hidden from the public and performed in the privacy of a team's practice or written in the secrecy of a locker room. Prior to

Figure 2.9. In this photo taken during Auburn's 2008 match-up against the University of Georgia, Auburn lines up in its traditional defensive formation: four linemen (DE, short for defensive end, and DT, short for defensive tackle) and three linebackers (W, M, and S). The SS, creeping close to the line of scrimmage, is not counted in a four-three formation. The position of the linemen is not given in Cov. 4 Play Action. (Photo taken by author.)

public embodiment, these texts are guarded carefully, yet, paradoxically, have no present, only future, value. A team does not win a game simply by sketching a creative and innovative play, circulating it solely in their narrow community of practice.

Auburn's Cov. 4 Play Action works from a four-three base defense formation in which there are four defensive linemen and three linebackers. Auburn needs a talented Mike to run effectively a four-three defense. A four-three highlights a team's linebacking core, especially Mike, instead of having to rely on the combined strength of four linebackers, which a three-four defense contains. Auburn has traditionally organized its defense in this four-three formation, and typically a head coach works from a consistent defensive formation. In figure 2.9, four defensive linemen (DTs and DEs) are lined up on the line of scrimmage while three linebackers (W, M, and S) are stacked roughly three to five yards behind the line of scrimmage. A Cover 4 also highlights Auburn's roster strengths and attempts to mask some roster shortcomings. With a young group of defensive backs, bolstered by future NFL first-round pick Carlos Rogers, Auburn worked from a Cover 4 alignment. This alignment divides the field into quarters, which is helpful because it does not place a young and inexperienced defensive back one on one against a receiver. A Cover 4 is also helpful in stopping the run and play actions, both of which are favorite offensive plays in the run-heavy SEC conference.

During a game, these plays move from being impotent yet complex texts to effective and public performances of the text. Embodiment not only moves these texts from the private to public sphere, but embodiment gauges the effectiveness of these plays. Again, it does not matter whether a play looks good on paper or on a placard; it matters whether the play can be properly embodied by the players.

Syverson's (1999) argument adds an additional wrinkle to embodiment. She holds that "writers, readers, and texts have physical bodies and consequently not only the content but the process of their interaction is dependent on, and reflective of, physical experience" (12). I agree texts have physical bodies, as I can think of how words look on a page gives me a certain physical reaction, how a certain color ink, a font, the weight of a book impact my physical relationship to the text. If this holds, then we need to consider how a football play itself has an embodied presence. The question, then, is how a play's embodiment interacts with a football player's embodiment, or more specifically, how embodiment circulates from text to player and back again. I am curious about how a single embodied play circulates across various semiotic resources. As issues surrounding circulation continue to animate our field (see, Gries 2013; 2015), it is worth examining how football has constructed an extracurricular community of practice in which embodiment is effectively circulated across several iterations of a text to a person in less than thirty-five seconds and in which this circulation rarely breaks down. During the course of a game, teams run upwards of one hundred total offensive and defensive plays. In all these plays, embodiment is circulated.[7] Again, we can conceptualize via Syverson how a text is embodied; however, the embodiment of such a text is not assessed until the text is embodied by a football player. Moreover, through embodying these plays, the line between text and body fades.

Figure 2.10 comes from a 2013 match-up between West Virginia and Oklahoma held in Norman, Oklahoma. On his belt, the West Virginia defensive player wears the defensive plays he will embody. Though the text is illegible, the plays are divided into four equally sized, color-coded squares. The plays on his belt work in a liminal zone between abstract and concrete representation as the play oscillates from textual to bodily representation. It's a curious use of text in that the two—the play as text and the play as the bodily enactment—carry the same information yet do so through different mediums. Like musical notes or lines in a screenplay existing as visually scripted text but intended for bodily delivery, the plays on the belt and the embodied performance carry the same information—telling the defensive player where to stand, whom to defend. The two, however, are not redundant. The play as text hanging from the player's belt relies on alphabetic and numeric text and color to remind the player of the particular play signaled from the sideline. The

Figure 2.10. A defensive player for West Virginia with the plays on his waist. (Photo by Valorie Wakefield. Used with permission.)

two layers of text (the play as text and the play as the body) blur together in a performative action. The efficacy of these plays as text relies on the bodily performance, not the textual inscription. Poor play often results in adjusting the bodily enactment, not rewriting the plays as text.

Just as the sofa cushions represented the body for Jason during the locker-room demonstration at Auburn I detailed in chapter 1, the vast constellation of modes within a college football play represent a body or dictate how a body should be oriented. In West Virginia's Reo 37, shapes represent the defensive players; alphabetic text and the curious symbolic sign *$$* represent either a specific player (such as *QB* for the quarterback) or provide direction for the player to embody during the enactment of the play (such as *X-Block Man Over*, as seen in the text box). Even the dashed and solid, angled and straight lines represent how a player should physically orient himself on the field and which direction he should move his body once the referee blows the whistlc to signal a play's beginning. All text responds to the embodied experience and embodied potential of the player; all text directly represents a player and dictates his movement for the next several seconds. Kathryn Perry's (2012) question regarding the line between the physical and conceptual during composing signals attention to how the two are intertwined during meaning's representation in a college-football play. This intertwining is unique to college football. As I type these words on my aged, black Dell keyboard, each alphabetic character I produce does not directly represent or signify a person; the rhetorical analyses, memos, tweets, and blogs my writing students compose during a semester do not often signify a person. The representation of meaning within a football play points to the body and signifies the person and dictates the person's immediate physical action. Thus, the play's potential and limitations hinge on a person's ability to embody and then deliver the text.

Representative of Stephen Witte's (1992) understanding of a "text" as an "organized set of symbols or signs" (237), these plays evince the writing practices of our student-athletes. Basketball and football are complex literate activities imbued with a great variety of practices beyond the enactment of the playbook. And this is a mode of writing that resonates with how current scholars and professional organizations conceptualize writing, though composition studies and the larger field of English studies has long ignored the athletic part of the university experience. In her NCTE presidential address, Kathleen Blake Yancey (2008) noted that "we have multiple modes of composing operating simultaneously" (331). Plays, with their deconstruction of a hierarchical system of meaning making (i.e., alphabetic text dominant over image, sound, and other modes), adhere to Yancey's vision of the New Age of Composition. Scripted sports plays also align with how Andrea Lunsford (2006) recasts writing in her Computers and Writing Conference keynote. Lunsford sees writing as "epistemic, performative, multivocal, multimodal, and multimediated" (171). Football and basketball plays are performative; they entail the coherence of multiple voices and multiple modes. In addition, in the NCTE's 2004 position statement "Professional Knowledge for the Teaching of Writing" (National Council of Teachers of English 2004), the Executive Committee provides a section titled "Composing Occurs in Different Modalities and Technologies." They assert that "as basic tools for communicating expand to include modes beyond print alone, 'writing' comes to mean more than scratching words with pen and paper." Though the NCTE statement is largely concerned with classroom practice and the multitude of modes and composing choices at a writer's disposal with the development of technology, the emphasis on what writing means, the nod toward the unlimited possibilities of what writing is and can be, resonates when viewing plays as writing. When our leading scholars and professional organizations increasingly push for a larger understanding of what counts as writing and argue for an understanding and acknowledgment of extracurricular writing, room is open for an examination of plays as an instantiation of writing worthy of attention.

So what are plays and what do they? I return to my definition: plays are multimodal texts, dialectically constructed, historically situated. They *do* by anticipating competitive bodily action through undergoing resemiotization and then being embodied by players.

In short, plays are writing that does action.

* * *

Sitting in Auburn's Jordan-Hare Stadium with my wife that November day in 2008—disappointed Auburn came up short against their rival Georgia Bulldogs—I watched the Tigers embody Cov. 4 Play Action. I finished my MA the next season and sat in my living room late one January night as the Tigers won the national championship. I watched many of the players I taught in FYC and supervised during mandatory study hours rush the field, helmets in hands, jubilee spread on their faces. And my thoughts returned—as they periodically do—to the highly regarded wide receiver, Trey, who composed his essay on Notepad that hot summer in the library and left Auburn just the season before the national championship season. I thought of how Trey learned and enacted hundreds of offensive plays, how he could talk and walk me through the nuances of movement, how he could read his opponent's bodily movements, how he could interpret his spatial orientation on the field in relation to his opponent. He succeeded on the field and struggled in the classroom. The classroom struggles won out and he left school.

I'm not lamenting the primacy of athletics over academics. But if we are sincere in our scholarship addressing multimodality, delivery, circulation, and embodiment, then the next time we find college sports on television, we would do well to watch closely and ask ourselves the following: how do these players, the players who we are told should struggle in our class and any class, publicly embody multimodal plays as texts, and what do they teach us about what writing is and how it's accomplished? These are the high-profile student-athletes on our campuses, interviewed by ESPN, pasted on the cover of *Sports Illustrated*, known and discussed on a national level, and the ones who have a great deal to teach *us* about the role of the body in writing. To learn from these student-athletes, I turn to them more directly in the next chapter and allow them to speak of their sport, their plays, and their writing.

Notes

1. A portion of this chapter was published as "Writing as Embodied, College Football Plays as Embodied: Extracurricular Multimodal Composing" (Rifenburg 2014) in *Composition Forum*. Article reprinted with permission from *Composition Forum*: www. compositionforum.com.

2. Streaming underneath my argument in this chapter is a current of conversation regarding copyright and scripted plays. I collected these plays at the same time NCTE tasked me and three other colleagues with revising the CCCC Guidelines for the Ethical Conduct of Research in Composition Studies; therefore, my thoughts often turned to ownership of scripted plays during data collection. In this chapter, I include endnotes detailing my attempt to locate ownership of and permission to use these plays. Despite increased attention and importance placed on intellectual property in the wake of the digital era and the dissemination of discourses across innumerable digital platforms, I have yet to find consensus on the ownership of scripted sports plays. The framers of the US Constitution granted Congress the power to enact copyright legislation: "Congress shall have Power . . . to promote the Progress of Science and useful Arts, by securing for limited Times to Authors and Inventors the exclusive Right to their respective Writings and Discoveries" (US Constitution art. I, § 8, cl. 8). The Supreme Court and federal circuit courts cases clarified opaque phrases in the Constitution, such as "useful Arts" and "Discoveries." And the US copyright laws of 1909 and 1976 further advanced copyright understandings. The 1976 law, in brief, reads, "Copyright protection subsists, in accordance with this title, in original works of authorship fixed in any tangible medium of expression, now known or later developed, from which they can be perceived, reproduced, or otherwise communicated, either directly or with the aid of a machine or device" (17 U.S.C. § 102(a)). The law then states the eight categories of authorship, which include "pantomimes and choreographic works." Through this category, copyright law, patents, and trademarks have been extended to elements of bodily arts and some elements of competitive sports. For example, the choreographer George Balanchine filed suit over the dissemination of images of his choreography for *The Nutcracker*. In *Horgan v. MacMillan* (1986; 789 F. 2d 517 [2d Cir.])), the US States Court of Appeals for the Second Circuit ruled in favor of Balanchine vis-à-vis Horgan (the executrix of Balanchine's estate), setting precedent for future copyright extension to other choreographed works. But the court has yet to render a decision on scripted sports plays despite many law articles arguing for the extension of copyright protection to scripted plays (see, for example, Das 2000; Kieff, Kramer, and Kunstadt 2008; Moberg, 2004). My reading leads me to believe I do not need to seek permission to reprint scripted plays—though seeking such permission would be courteous to the key stakeholders and in line with the CCCC Guidelines for the Ethical Conduct of Research in Composition Studies statement, a curious case in which the ethics for research in composition studies goes above legal requirements (National Council of Teachers of English 2015). However, when possible, I attempted to locate the original author of the scripted play for permission. I blogged about issues related to copyright and scripted plays in more depth on my website: mrifenburg.wordpress.com.

3. The Auburn playbook has the name of then-defensive line coach Don Dunn written across the title page. At the time of my writing this endnote, Dunn is coaching at Western Kentucky. Who, then, owns these plays—Auburn or Dunn? The employer or the employee? I started with Auburn. I called a special-collections librarian and archivist. My query stumped the archivist. He passed on the name and number of Auburn's legal counsel. I left a voicemail and received a call back several hours

later. Counsel said Auburn doesn't have any claim to the playbook. The playbook was over ten years old, written by a former coach (Dunn) for a former head coach (Tommy Tubberville, now at Cincinnati). I then called an administrative assistant with the athletics department at Western Kentucky. She referred me to the director of media relations for football. A voicemail, an e-mail, and a tweet later, I connected with the director. We spoke over the phone, exchanged more tweets, and I tried to explain my work. Eventually, after I e-mailed a portion of my book, I received an e-mail from the director saying Dunn approved my use of the play.

4.   The permission process was more streamlined with this play. I e-mailed the associate general counsel at West Virginia to inquire into using scripted plays from the playbook. Counsel responded: "The University has no objections to the use of the image from the publically available 2005 playbook." The adverb *publicly* is important when considering who owns scripted plays and intellectual property issues. I do wonder whether I would have received a different response if the head coach who authored the playbook (Rodriguez) was still employed by the school.

5.   My use of iconic signs and my later use of symbolic signs follows the lead of M. Jimmie Killingsworth and Michael K. Gilbertson. Killingsworth and Gilbertson (1992) define an iconic sign as an image that constructs an analogous resemblance to an object. An example would be an image of a file folder on a computer screen *iconically* representing electronic documents stored on the computer. Symbolic signs, on the other hand, "bear an arbitrary relation" to a referent "based on a law or agreement" (50).

6.   Unfortunately, I did not locate a date for the Arizona State play.

7.   One strand of research to consider regarding circulation studies and scripted sports plays is how some texts go viral and others do not. In her award-winning book *Still Life with Rhetoric: A New Materialist Approach for Visual Rhetoric* (2015), Laurie E. Gries reports data from her five-year case study on the digital circulation of the iconic image Obama Hope, designed by Shepard Fairey and used in Barack Obama's successful 2008 presidential campaign. At the core of Gries's detailed case study is her commitment to studying how images spread and go viral. She helpfully contributes a definition of *going viral*—a phrase creeping close to an empty signifier—by offering that "we reserve the descriptor *going viral* for things that are highly mobile, contagious, replicable, metacultural, and reflexive" (Gries 2015, 285). Building on this stipulative definition, she suggests in her conclusion that "we can learn to spread our messages more widely by thinking more carefully about how circulation unfolds in a digital age and making delivery a forethought in our composing practices" (Gries 2015, 285). Though I do not think college football and basketball coaches seek for their plays to *go viral* across various digital platforms, they do focus on spreading their message, their plays. These plays need to spread across all members of the team: from the head coach, to the many assistant and graduate-assistant coaches, from the seniors on the team all the way down to the walk-on first-year players. The NCAA allows 105 players on a football roster. Add in the many different kinds and levels of coaches, and the number of people who need to receive the circulating plays goes higher. However, for these plays to be rhetorically effective they cannot be spread beyond their immediate audiences. Gries's study of the spread of Obama Hope is furthered by the pervasive presence of the image across the world and across a multitude of semiotic resources. Obama Hope is rhetorically active and effective because of its pervasive presence. A close reading of college football and basketball plays alongside Obama Hope asks how text becomes rhetorically active and effective and how a text spreads yet stops once it has reached the intended audience. In other words, how does a text go viral only a little?

3

HOW DO OUR STUDENT-ATHLETES LEARN PLAYS?
A Case Study of a Division II Men's Basketball Team

The most athletic guys learn by doing. They don't learn by looking at it in a playbook or looking at it drawn up on a whiteboard.
> —University of North Georgia head basketball coach Chris Faulkner

[Running a play] is more muscle-memory-it. You hear the play, and it triggers something in you and you go.
> —University of North Georgia senior guard Travis Core

Performing textual analysis of plays taken from four hundred-plus-page playbooks, as I did in the previous chapter, paints just a portion of the picture of the writing practices of our student-athletes.[1] To see fully these writing practices, I look at how student-athletes engage with these complex playbooks. Seeing and knowing our students is at the heart of our field. As Patricia Bizzell (2014) writes in her apologia for composition studies to the wide-ranging readership of *PMLA*, "We in this field want to know who our students are" (442). I needed to set aside for a moment the mountains of text and attend practice, sit on the bench, and talk with the players. I had to get to know our student-athletes. I worked with players at Auburn and Oklahoma, but I never gained first-person access to how coaches and players coauthor plays. I gained this access at the University of North Georgia (UNG).

During the 2014–2015 basketball season, I embedded myself in the men's basketball team at UNG, a Division II school with a roughly $3 million annual athletic budget competing in the Peach Belt Conference (PBC). Unlike many Division I schools—Rutgers most notably—UNG operates in the black each year. Its budget is composed of endowments,

DOI: 10.7330/9781607326892.c003

annual giving, and student fees. These fees are prorated based on the number of credit hours the student is taking. During the 2014–2015 academic year, the athletics department directed $1,005,858 to scholarships for many of their 225 student-athletes. Compared to their fellow PBC schools, UNG ranks second to last in how much money they direct toward scholarships, which is officially termed "scholarship equivalency." The NCAA allocates the number of scholarships a school may give per sport. For basketball, the NCAA allows Division II schools ten scholarships. The majority of Division I schools fund all their NCAA-allocated scholarships. The majority of Division II schools do not because they don't have the money. There are no scholarships for the Division III level. During the 2014–2015 season, UNG scholarship equivalency was 57 percent, twelfth out of fourteen schools in their conference. Despite their low budget, UNG athletics has found success; most notably, their softball team won the Division II national championship in 2015.

Through the support of the faculty athletics representative, the athletics director, and the head basketball coach, I attended practices, traveled with the team, sat on the bench during games, and listened in on film sessions and locker-room talks. The athletics director, Lindsey Reeves, granted me access to the coaching staff and players. Head coach Chris Faulkner shared scouting-reports (see fig. 3.5) and handwritten miscellany and texted me screenshots of notes he wrote on his iPhone (see fig. 3.6). Assistant coaches Josh Travis, Jared Hawkins, Richard Simmons, and Brian Cole answered my many questions. I interviewed players in my office and watched them talk me through plays they drew.[2] Throughout the season, I focused on how Faulkner and his staff teach, and players learn, plays.

My argument is direct: my data suggest players learn the complex plays of their community of practice through three cognitive processes—spatial orientation, haptic communication, and scaffolded situations. Just like the players who embodied plays I analyzed in chapter 2, the men's basketball players at UNG develop a method for understanding, internalizing, and enacting a bodily literacy for their community of practice.

I offer a first-person narrative of the season, a rich picture of the many practices, games, and hallway and office conversations I had with the coaching staff and players. I follow the team from their practices in early November to the raw, February night—such bad conditions that Georgia's governor declared a state of emergency—when the team lost at home and, with the defeat, was eliminated from postseason play. At the close, I elaborate on spatial orientation, haptic communication, and scaffolded situations. These cognitive processes are grounded in recent research speaking generally to learning theory and more specifically to the connection among the mind, the body, and external objects during cognitive activity. I draw from Nedra Reynolds's (2004) work highlighting the role of location in writing, Laura Micciche's (2014) work in what she terms "new materialism," and Isabelle Thompson's (2009) work on scaffolding during writing center tutoring sessions. I suggest that the cognitive processes of spatial orientation, haptic communication, and scaffolded situations collectively illustrate that engaging with and learning plays demands engaging and learning through the body. Moreover, these three ways speak to the larger question driving this book: how do student-athletes know?

As I drafted this chapter, my mind often returned to a conversation I had early in the season with Faulkner. We were riding the team's bus to an away game in Morrow, Georgia, and Faulkner was explaining what he tries to teach on offense: "I can't tell you exactly what is going to happen [when my players run a play]. Where some coaches will tell you that 'Okay, when we throw it here, this guy is going to cut here, and do this, this, and this,' we don't do that. . . . Well, obviously, there are set plays where everything is manipulated, but most of the time it is a freelance type of thing."[3] Student-athletes achieve this balance between freelancing and manipulating by attending to their location in regards to others, coordinating meaning with others and objects through their senses, particularly touch, and encouraging the sequential building of skills. In other words, they learn through spatial orientation, haptic communication, and scaffolded situations.

CHRIS FAULKNER'S COACHING PHILOSOPHY

Since 2003, Chris Faulkner has coached the University of North Georgia Nighthawks, accumulating a near .500 record. He played at UNG—then North Georgia College—from 1989 to 1993 and landed the head-coaching job at Piedmont College before taking the reins at his alma mater. When Faulkner returned to UNG, the team competed in the less prestigious National Association of Intercollegiate Athletics. During his second year, the NCAA granted the Nighthawks Division II status. The team now competes in the Peach Belt Conference against schools in Alabama, Florida, South Carolina, and North Carolina. During the 2014–2015 season, Faulkner's staff included assistant coaches Josh Travis and Richard Simmons and graduate-assistant coaches Jared Hawkins and Brian Cole.

Like all coaches, Faulkner has a particular coaching style and offensive and defensive philosophy dictating the types of players he needs to

Player	Position	Year	Height	Weight	Hometown
Sean Brennan	Guard	Sophomore	6-2	168	Roswell, GA
Jesse Byrd	Guard	Freshman	6-0	155	Decatur, GA
Tyler Dominy	Guard	Freshman	6-5	191	Dawsonville, GA
Taylor Guthrie	Guard	Junior	6-4	183	Dahlonega, GA
Corey Green	Forward	Junior	6-4	209	Detroit, MI
Tanner Plemmons	Guard	Junior	6-2	188	Franklin, NC
Shaquan Cantrell	Guard	Sophomore	6-4	195	Gainesville, GA
Ebo Smith	Guard	Freshman	6-3	177	Lula, GA
Travis Core	Guard	Senior	6-2	167	Trenton, GA
T.J. Williams	Forward	Sophomore	6-8	240	Wilmington, NC
Dylen Setzekorn	Forward	Junior	6-7	194	Gainesville, GA
Andrew Lawrence	Forward	Senior	6-6	198	Hilliard, FL
Michael Varrichione	Forward	Junior	6-6	220	Medway, MA

Figure 3.1. UNG's roster for the 2014–2015 season.

recruit. Indicative of his style is a story he told me early in the season. During practice, Faulkner told me, Travis arranged five players in a unique offensive formation. He then pointed to five other players and told them to find a way to guard against the formation. The players looked unsure and tentatively arranged themselves on the court for a few moments. Simmons tried to add more verbal direction, but Faulkner called him off. The coaches stood by as the defenders adapted to the odd alignment. Allowing players freedom to "figure things out on their own" is central to Faulkner's coaching style. "As far as on the court, we give them a framework as to how to play and let them play within that. We are not where you have to stand here, you gotta do this, you gotta do that," Faulkner says. "I want to give them the freedom to read things: 'Okay, my defender did this, so I can do this.' Some of our new guys are struggling with that." In his office, Faulkner mentioned starting point Sean Brennan, a transfer from a Division I program, struggling with the freedom in Faulkner's system.[4] "It is almost discovery learning," Faulkner said about his coaching philosophy. He wants players to learn on their own how plays work by moving their bodies through the play and also watching it unfold on film. "I think that if they think they discover it, they think it is right more so than if I tell them," he said with a chuckle. "They place more value on it that way."

Even though he stresses discovery learning, basketball is a team sport that would fall apart without clear, agreeable objectives. "But there is a framework" to the offense, Faulkner insists. In general, this framework, his offensive philosophy, is spreading the floor by having four players who can shoot well, particularly a high-percentage three-pointer. Shooting a high percentage from behind the three-point line causes the defense to expand to defend the outside shot. By expanding, the defense opens up driving lanes to the basket for the offense. To enact his philosophy through plays, Faulkner relies on hand signals and verbal cues, as do football coaches, to transmit plays during a game: "Everything has a verbal call and got a name to it. Everything has a hand signal, as well. We got Up, Ear, Chin, Elbow." Faulkner points to the corresponding parts of his body as he rattles off his common offensive plays. He largely uses these verbal cues and hand signals to script in-bounds plays and when the team is looking a bit disorganized and in need of direction. During timeouts, Faulkner scripts plays on a whiteboard with a black marker.

In the games I observed, Faulkner always went to this whiteboard and marker during a media timeout. During the majority of the games, however, Faulkner looks for his point guard to dictate the flow of action and call plays with the same verbal cues and hand signals. As Brennan describes it, we "kinda go with the flow and when we need something specific he [Faulkner] will call a play." Brennan continues, "It usually would be when I get a feel for the game and how people are playing certain people [that I call a play]. And if I feel T. J. [Williams, the starting center] could get an easy seal on a guy, I might run Ear. Or if he has a height or strength advantage, I would run Ear. If Ebo [Smith, a guard] or Tanner [Plemmons, a guard] haven't really gotten the ball or gotten into rhythm yet, I might call Elbow, so they can come off [a screen] and make decisions, like get involved, things like that."

Defensively, Faulkner sticks to man-to-man. He has coached a press defense, a formation designed to guard the offense immediately after the offense in-bounds rather than waiting for the offense to dribble into the defense's half of the court. Faulkner color codes his press defense (red, green, yellow). Green directs the defense to trap (i.e., surround) the player who receives the first in-bound pass; yellow gives the players

Figure 3.2. Faulkner diagramming a play against Clayton State. (Photo taken by author.)

the option to trap; red is not trapping. He also signals the press with a closed fist. A closed fist held high means a full-court press. A closed fist held by the waist means a half-court press. Together, he might signal a green full-court press, meaning his team immediately traps at full court.

PRACTICE

NOVEMBER 7TH, 2014

In the 2014–2015 preseason poll, Peach Belt Conference coaches picked Faulkner's squad to finish a disappointing eighth out of fourteen teams in the conference. The first game against Southern Wesleyan University is just over a week away. Faulkner stands in the center of the court staring at sheets of papers, periodically looking at the surrounding action. Earlier he told me he planned for a short, easy practice. He blows his whistle at 3:07 p.m., and the team huddles around him. Basketballs quiet fast. He provides an overview of the practice and the team breaks with a collective shout of "One . . . two . . . three . . . Hard work!"

The coaches run the players through a five on zero transition: five players on offensive without defenders. Faulkner tells his players to emphasize the dribble drag both ways. Travis throws the ball against the backboard.

A player rebounds the ball and leads a fast break in the opposite direction. The drill has only three minutes left. The players and the ball are whipping around the court with the frenzied sounds of the bounce of the ball and the squeak of rubber-soled shoes. Suddenly, Faulkner sees something he doesn't like. He blows his whistle. Players stop.

Faulkner walks over to the players and picks up the ball. He says he was thinking about this play last night and then watching how players ran it today. He takes sophomore guard Shaquan Cantrell by the elbow and moves him slightly. "I don't think we need to screen him [the defender]. I think we can just cut," Faulkner says. The players are breathing heavily but listening and nodding.

Senior Travis Core suggests also adding that adjustment to a different play. Faulkner agrees and makes the change to that play. Faulkner does not inscribe these changes into a document or even scribble them on a loose sheet of paper. The impetus for this change arose from Faulkner watching how his players physically moved through the play during practice. By physically moving players around him, he saw the efficacy of such an adjustment. A player spoke up and suggested an amendment to a different play, and Faulkner granted the amendment.

The whistle blows. The drill begins again. UNG beats Southern Wesleyan eight days later.

PRACTICE
DECEMBER 2ND, 2014

The Nighthawks find themselves at 5–1 after a successful Thanksgiving break tournament in Pensacola, Florida, where the team beat Chowan University and Claflin University. The team now has two weeks off before their next game. College coaches have long pointed to the period between Thanksgiving break and the start of the spring semester as a time when teams either come together or fall apart. "I always look at it like this is the time where we've got a lot of our stuff in, but now's the time where we really try to refine it and get even better at it. And add other pieces of what you want to put in, as well," Faulkner tells me. Once finals are over and most students leave campus, the basketball team forms a tighter bond unencumbered by class schedules, final exams, and the social life that comes with living on a college campus. Without additional demands, teams find themselves focusing only on basketball on a largely deserted campus. During the winter break, the NCAA does not enforce the rule restricting teams to twenty practice hours a week. And because most teams have played quality nonconference opponents and competed in a Thanksgiving tournament, coaches are aware of their team's strengths and weaknesses. The winter break is a chance to hit the restart button on the season or refine what is already working well. Once the calendar turns, conference play begins and the slow march to March (the time of conference and NCAA tournaments) proceeds.

Faulkner looks deep in thought as he walks across his newly polished court, his head down and his teeth gnawing on his whistle. Around him, players are loosening up before the 3:30 p.m. small-group practice. Because of class schedules, Faulkner holds two small-group practices and then a whole-team practice later in the day. Today's practice will run half the team through the five on zero UP series, a series of offensive plays in which the power forward and center are positioned up by the free-throw line. Without a defense, five players will run through several different plays shouted by Faulkner as he crouches in midcourt and watches: "Elbow," "Ear," "Rub," "Chin." The players run through the plays, adding slight modifications to each. One time, Brennan might roll one direction off the ball screen; another time, Brennan might roll the other direction and look to send a bounce pass to Williams on the block. The players move quickly through the plays. Faulkner's voice cuts through the quiet: "Go again." "Go again." "Do it again."

Something goes wrong with an unfolding play, and Faulkner rises from his knee at half court and makes his way to the free-throw line. He is chewing gum and rubbing his temple as he walks. He doesn't shout and gesticulate wildly like some coaches. Faulkner is reserved, almost quiet. He has a soft complexion that belies his age and a soft voice, not the raspy, intense voice you would expect of a college head coach who yells for a living. When you talk to him, he listens. He slows down and meets your eyes. Some coaches are high energy, always moving. Not Faulkner. Maybe it is the slower pace of the mountain community of Dahlonega, Georgia, or that the pressures of Division II Peach Belt Conference basketball are not as acute as, say, Division I ACC basketball, but for whatever reason, Faulkner doesn't come off as your typical coach. He wants to listen and learn.

Faulkner takes junior forward Mike Varrichione by the elbow. Moving Varrichione around, Faulkner points out that he wants Varrichione to move during screen. "Gotta get your mind just right," he says. Faulkner blows his whistle, and the play begins again.

In a game, the points are what is important and what people notice. However, at this small-group practice, coaches and players emphasize orienting a body within the unfolding play. Faulkner and the assistant coaches aren't watching whether the ball goes through the net. Their eyes don't follow the ball's arc once released from a player's hands. Coaches watch players move within the half-court offense, how players move with and against each other, and how they embody the scripted plays. During a game, coaches design a play to lead to a made basket within the thirty-five-second shot clock. During practice, coaches slow a play down, tease it apart, and critique it to help student-athletes learn.

Traditional signs of literacy designed to aid in this learning are largely absent. Faulkner does type a schedule on UNG basketball letterhead before each practice. This schedule details the types and durations of drills. Periodically, at the bottom of the schedule, Faulkner provides notes, such as "Community Service tomorrow @ 5:00PM" and "Film Times Tomorrow." Faulkner gives several copies of the practice schedule to the other coaches. Simmons is the only one who spends much time looking it over, tenderly folding it into quarters and tucking it into his back pocket. During one practice, Simmons borrows my pen to jot notes onto the schedule (the coaches don't carry pens, clipboards, or dry-erase boards). Other than the schedule, no physical texts circulate. Faulkner doesn't have a whiteboard on wheels sitting off to the side. He doesn't have a whiteboard imposed on a clipboard as he does during a game. None of the coaches carries pens or other writing technologies. I have yet to see Faulkner write anything during practice, even the ephemeral notation. The team doesn't even have a physical playbook. Despite the rise of tablets and migrating physical playbooks onto tablets, none of the coaches takes advantage of digital technology to teach during practice. Faulkner does have a list of "everything we run" stored on his computer, and the athletics department does pay a yearly fee for access to a common software called FastDraw, which allows users to diagram and share plays digitally. Yet none of the players I spoke with knew of FastDraw.

Faulkner is also text-free during a game. The assistant coaches, however, busily take notes and construct text to analyze team and opponent performance. Travis charts fouls, timeouts, and the opposing team's shooting statistics. Hawkins charts defensive efficiency, and Cole charts offensive efficiency. Simmons charts four-minute games by breaking up the full forty-minute game into ten four-minute periods and tallying the score at the end of each four-minute period to visualize trends in the game. Yet Faulkner told me once with a wry smile that he rarely looks at these charts. I never saw Faulkner show his players the data charted by his coaching staff though he did refer to some specific stats taken from these charts during pregame, postgame, and halftime talks.

None of the players I spoke with voiced concern about lack of a physical text, particularly a playbook, and none believed having one would improve the team's performance. As Travis Core explained, "I think it [a playbook] makes you robotic. I think it makes you say 'Okay, you are X, you run here.' And really in a game your plays don't look like that anyway. They are designed to set you up to be successful, but if you break away from the play a little bit and do something really good, that is better than running the play in general." Even though Williams had a playbook in high school, he agreed: "I guess if you paid attention in practice and actually were part of the drills and went through it at game speed you catch on, you remember it." Core even went so far to say that Faulkner has expressed frustration with players before for following a play too closely: "I know he yells at us sometimes for running the play robotically. Like you know, we run the plays to get you guys open, if you are open doing it a little differently, do it." The comments by Core and Williams reflect Faulkner's overarching philosophy of balancing manipulation of action with freelancing.

The players I spoke with did not believe a physical playbook would help them remember all the complex plays they run. Williams admitted he sometimes forgets how to run a play during a game. To trigger his memory, he relies on how others—defenders and teammates—orient themselves to help kick-start his muscle memory: "When they move, you know that the spot that they just moved from is where you are supposed to be or in the general area. Like if someone is near me I will be like 'Oh, crap, I gotta set a screen for them.' I feel like that happens some-times. Because of the speed of the game sometimes you might call some-thing and be like 'uh' and taking a minute and then you go right into it."

Core's experience is similar. For the past several years, he ran the point-guard position. With Brennan transferring onto the team this season, Core found himself playing shooting guard and running off the ball while Brennan handled the point: "Because I am usually seeing it from the one [the point-guard position] and then when he [Brennan] calls the play I am like 'uh' and then I am 'Okay, there we go.' And that is definitely why I think the playbook doesn't do so much for me per-sonally. It is more muscle-memory-it. You hear the play, and it triggers something in you and you go."

I appreciate how Core turned *muscle memory* into a verb. For him, it is an action in which he orients his body in relation to others within the ever-shifting play. Drew Lawrence, a senior on the team, also talked of external objects—such as players and locations on the court—triggering his muscle memory of a play he may forget: "Sometimes you are able to talk yourself through it. Sometimes you are able to pick it up about half-way through and go from faking to actually remembering what you are

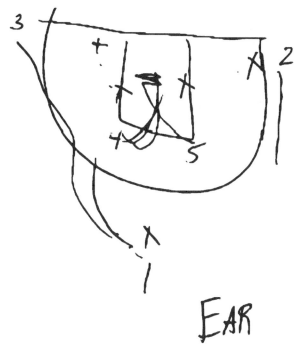

Figure 3.3. Sophomore guard Sean Brennan's drawing of the offensive play Ear.

actually supposed to be doing and can get right there. And sometimes you just blank out and think 'crap, I just forgot what I am supposed to do?' The way the point guard calls it and things you see out of your peripheral could jumpstart something." Lawrence does acknowledge that sometimes you "just blank out"—later he tells me sometimes he "fakes it 'til I make it." That said, Lawrence has the experience to weave his body into an unfolding play he may not fully remember by seeing things "out of [his] peripheral."

These players know the plays through their bodies and only periodically recognize textual representations of the plays. In my office, I gave Brennan a white sheet of printer paper and a blue pen. I asked him to draw me a play the team runs. He drew and labeled the play *Ear*.

When I sat down the next day with Lawrence, I slid Brennan's drawing across my desk and asked him whether he recognized the play. Lawrence, a senior who has played on the team for three years, didn't recognize the play. Maybe it was the way Brennan drew the play or seeing the play out of context (i.e., in my office), but Lawrence blanked. During the course of our interview, he—without my prodding—returned to Brennan's drawing, snatching it and looking at it and again stating his confusion. "I should probably go over that. I should say, 'Hey, Coach, what's Ear?" he said at one point with a laugh. When I concluded the interview, he returned to Brennan's drawing. As he stood, he said, "I probably remember most of them just by where we are trying to get the ball to. If I remember right, Ear is probably trying to get it to the post. It might be Up Ear. That might be why I am not remembering it." Lawrence was right. It just took him thirty minutes to remember.

Lawrence and his teammates immerse themselves in text. Their bodies either disseminate or enact this text through physical movement or verbal and gestural play signaling. When a player doesn't run a play correctly, Faulkner or an assistant coach take the player, move him in the right direction, and point out the play's nuances as teammates watch. College basketball is a highly discursive space where bodies are continually enacting a textual play. This continual enactment illustrative of what Knoblauch (2012) refers to as "embodied knowledge" in her delineation of approaches to embodiment. Knoblauch describes embodied knowledge as "knowledge . . . very clearly connected to the body" (Knoblauch 2012, 54). As an example, she states her assurance that if she thinks about something too much (like an online password) she will not be able to remember it, but her fingers will as they fly across the keyboard. Physicality and the body are both vehicles for knowledge making. When the body is absent, such as when Lawrence looked at the textual representation of the play Ear, players struggle to know the play. They struggle to give voice to embodied knowledge.

PRACTICE
DECEMBER 10TH, 2014

I'm in the assistant coaches' office in the basement of the gym. Jared Hawkins and Josh Travis are weaving their hands through a seemingly endless loop of black wires. A forty-four-inch RCA projector television sits against the wall, and Hawkins is fiddling with AV outlets and an Xbox 360 sitting on a shelf above a Dell desktop computer. Two workers from plant operations are balancing on a ladder, weaving their hands through the black wires too. The workers removed a ceiling tile and are threading the wire along the rafters. The plan, Travis tells me, is to splice the Internet cable. Hawkins has aggregated game footage onto a private YouTube channel, which can be streamed via Xbox 360 live to the television. Since the television is so dated, it has taken creative electrical engineering to connect the desktop computer to the Xbox 360 to the television and splice the Internet cable to connect to both the Dell desktop and the Xbox 360. The Wi-Fi signal throughout campus is spotty, especially in the gym's basement. Once in place, players and coaches will be able to watch game film on the large television as opposed to on a desktop or laptop. There's even a couch, Travis tells me proudly, pointing to a dark red leather sofa lining the wall parallel to the computer. I see an Xbox controller wedged between two cushions.

Impressed by the ingenuity but disappointed by the vast discrepancy in resources from a Division I to a Division II program that makes such ingenuity necessary, I head out of the office, up the stairs, and into the gym to observe the afternoon practice. Graduation is two days away, and people are moving in heavy furniture and AV equipment to the stage in the gym, which will host graduation. In the background, players are running through their opening five on zero full-court offense.

Faulkner assumes his typical position: down on one knee in midcourt, chewing on his whistle. He blows his whistle and walks toward his players, his head down.

"Here's a little thing we want to put in on the fly for you, Shaq," he says, taking Shaquan Cantrell by the elbow. "Let's call this Zip 3. I don't think that will be too confusing."

Faulkner often physically moves his players through a specific formation. As Lawrence tells me, "Sometimes [Faulkner] might jump into my position if there are a couple of different options you can have and he wants to show you a couple different options. So if you are supposed to be reading something, he might grab you and say 'all right, let me get your spot for a second and let me show you what you are supposed to be doing.'"

Players are watching quietly as Faulkner introduces a new play. Zip 3 is not a completely new play. The basic formation and player movement are similar to other plays the team runs. Faulkner is building on the players' familiarity with the movement to add an additional option.

"What we are really trying to do is get the ball here," Faulkner says as he moves himself to a space on the court with the ball in his hand. "And look at all this space we got." He points to a roughly three-square-foot area of space on the court. Faulkner takes a couple steps. "Catch it here with a rip through, and Shaq attacking the goal right here. And we will run this for any guy in the [small forward] three spot."

Faulkner takes Cantrell's elbow again and moves him around ninety degrees. "Now go on this side of the screen. Everybody see this? Called *Zip 3*. Let's go through it right here." Faulkner blows his whistle and five players take off with the ball down the court. They run Zip 3. Faulkner verbally approves of their execution and calls on a different group of five. The players who were standing and watching Faulkner explain the play take off down the court. Several errant movements later, Faulkner blows his whistle, halting play.

"Okay, let's stop and look at this again," he says. "Ideally, we want you on this side of the floor." Faulkner takes Varrichione by the elbow and moves him slightly. While Faulkner moves Varrichione through the play, Drew raises his hand and asks a question I cannot hear, but I do hear Faulkner's reply, "Let's talk about that. Throw the ball to Corey [Green]."

When teaching plays, Faulkner is open to player feedback and questions. Williams, Core, and Lawrence told me they feel comfortable asking a question during a practice or in Faulkner's office. During my observation, I noted several times when Faulkner adjusted a play based on a question posed by a player. Faulkner is even open to his players disagreeing with his play calling, though that is a more delicate situation the players leave to Core and Lawrence, Williams tells me with a chuckle. As Williams says,

> If you didn't understand something or you think something might work better, [Faulkner] is always open to that. I mean like Travis [Core] does it a lot. Me being a big, setting screens for the guards, I might interject something. It's not a problem. I feel like if you got a high-level understanding for the game like you see something before it happens. So if you are running a play or practicing a play you be like, "If we run it this way, this will work." So you are like, "Coach, you sure we shouldn't do this?" or like "What exactly do you do like here?"

Core explains he has spoken against Faulkner's directives before. When he does, he does so understanding the complexity surrounding such a precarious rhetorical situation:

> I usually try to not to say it out loud. I usually try to come to the side and be like "I don't think this will put us in a very successful position." And I guess it helps I have been here for four years, and they know I have that relationship with them. But, yeah, I mean if I see something that I feel will put somebody in an uncomfortable position, I will voice my opinion about it, and they [the coaches] seem fairly comfortable. Because I don't come at them trying to undermine them or anything. It is more constructive, like "I think this will make it better." Obviously, they are not running the plays. We are. So we kinda have a feel for them.

Core signals strong awareness of the rhetorical situation he faces as a player questioning his coach's play calling. He pulls from his ethos to speak against a specific play and frames his dissent as "I don't think this [play] will put *us* in a very successful position." The plural pronoun *us* focuses attention on the needs of the collective team. Core also nods at a larger principle undergirding this chapter: players learn plays through the body. Core speaks against a particular play because it doesn't *feel* right. He knows coaches don't win games. Nor do creative and effective plays. As he told me during the season, "Players make plays." Core returns to this concept by highlighting that Faulkner, Travis, Simmons, and Hawkins are not running Up Ear. The players are. Through experience, the players feel which plays will be effective and which will not.

Core's comment also connects with Faulkner's desire to encourage discovery learning and the balance between manipulating a play and the "freelance type of thing." Through discovery learning, Core and his teammates feel when a play will not put them in successful positions. Instead of enforcing the play and dictating all court movement—as some coaches are apt to do—Faulkner allows the freelance type of thing, which opens space for players to interject a dissenting opinion.

Faulkner moves more players around as he teaches Zip 3. He blows his whistle and five players take off down the court. A thud issues from behind me as people place a fifty-pound lectern on the elevated stage.

CLAYTON STATE ROAD GAME
JANUARY 10TH, 2015

The team wins their next six games before heading to Morrow, Georgia, for a match-up against the Clayton State Lakers, one of the more athletic teams in the conference. The charter bus is idling as I pull into the parking lot early Saturday morning. I received a text from the faculty athletics representative, Margaret Poitevint, the night before. Since the men and women share a charter bus to away games, seats are at a premium.

We arrive at the gym an hour and a half before the women's scheduled tipoff. After dropping the women's team off, the bus takes us to Rocky's Café & Pizza, a family-owned restaurant. Travis tells me the team has been coming to Rocky's for years. He called ahead and the owner has a table and food waiting for us. During our meal, we order sandwiches that will be waiting for us when we swing by the restaurant on our way home.

Back at the gym, we are given a key to the visitor locker room. The key looks like one a teacher would give a middle-school student headed to the restroom. An eight-inch long block of wood hangs from the key. Written in black ink are the words "Guest Locker." I haven't visited other locker rooms within the conference, but coaches and players tell me Clayton State's facilities are near the bottom, as are UNG's. Preparing to enter the space, I can see why. The locker room is four concrete walls cordoning out a square space in the middle of a larger room. A room inside a room. The larger room appears to be a catchall space. Massive air-conditioning units are in one corner. Aged trophies and outdated advertising placards are in the other. Hard-back plastic chairs lie scattered about. I spot a dusty dictionary lying on the floor. Piping snakes around the exposed ceiling. The locker room itself is accessible via a flimsy wooden door. Inside, lockers and a dry-erase board line the walls.

Players change and film sessions begin. Hawkins downloads and clips video of opposing teams using a video editing program called GTX Hoops. The edited video shows several clips of each starting player for the opposition and offensive and defensive sets UNG predicts the opposition will run. Hawkins balances his black Dell laptop on a white plastic folding chair and uses an extension cord to reach the outlet. He then spaces out five more chairs in a semicircle around his laptop. Travis calls over the post players, and they take a seat. Standing behind the players, his arms folded across his chest, Travis talks the players through the clips Hawkins has aggregated. Travis tersely comments on opposition players' skills: "not a great outside shooter," "their most athletic player," "decent midrange." Locker-room banter is gone. The players are focused and ask periodic questions. The clips end, the players leave, and a new group sits down. Travis runs through the same video with the guards.

Restless minutes pass as the women's game drags. With less than six minutes in the game, Faulkner gathers his players in their locker room. With his suit jacket off and a green dry-erase marker in one hand and handwritten notes in the other, Faulkner reminds the team of yesterday's practice and the film they watched just a few minutes ago: "Real quick, I know you guys just watched film so this should be fresh on your mind. First of all, let me say this, when we are active on the defensive end of the floor, we are pretty dang good. And I think that was evidenced Wednesday night [in a win against Georgia Regents]. When we will get active and get five guys active and really involved defensively, that's when we are pretty dang good."

Faulkner weaves in a reminder of last year's game against Clayton State, a game UNG lost by two: "Last year at our place, they beat us and they beat us on the boards. And we have to do a great job of rebounding. They are very, very athletic across the board, and we gotta go and get bodies on them and make sure we are doing a good job rebounding."

Faulkner then moves to teaching more directly. He uncaps his marker and draws a quick outline of one half of a basketball court—just a circle for the basket and three sides of a rectangle for the paint—to help spatially orient his players to the forthcoming play. He adds dots for players and quick curved lines for routes the players will run. I have yet to see him draw anything in practice, and this is the first time I see Faulkner visually represent a play through drawing. The sketch is quick and messy. Faulkner says, "You have seen the flex-screen action. You walked through it in practice. You saw it on the video just now. A lot of different guys are cutting off the flex screen right there. We gotta make sure we don't get hit on the screen. . . . We gotta stay high side like we talked about yesterday in practice. T. J. [Williams] and Mike [Varrichione] you gotta be ready for that there. On ball screens and hand-offs, and you will see both, we treat them the same, right? Everybody is clear with what we are saying here?"

Assistant coach Josh Travis speaks up in the back of the room. He is the only other coach to speak during this important five-minute talk prior to tipoff. "Treat hand-offs like ball screens," he reminds the players. Faulkner continues. He immediately erases his first drawing with a rag and adds another. At no point does a scripted play or text stay on the board for more than several seconds: "Now really, guards, nothing really changes for you on a feather or a drag. Every thing's the same for you. It is really on the post players. So you guys need to be active and communicate that. If there is an empty situation, if this channel, and that thing is right in here and you don't know if it is a trap or a feather, it is at your discretion."

Faulkner's use of "discretion" signals his emphasis on discovery learning and allowing players the freedom to make decisions within his system He concludes by talking briefly about the plan for the opening minutes of the game and plays he intends to signal:

> We will go box defense on baseline out of bounds. We may go double fist some, as well. But know when we get like this [draws a formation], they are going to put shooter here, guy here with the ball, guy here signaling, big guy here. They will take this guy here and screen us and they will take this guy and go. You gotta get this guy to help over here. You all remember that? You saw it on the film. So now you should have a pretty good idea about what is going on with that. . . . Let's also remember that we talked yesterday about UP 45 and UP 54.

He ends with an exhortation echoed by some of the more vocal players like Varrichione. The team dismisses to start stretching. In the gym, the women are losing badly and the game is almost over. Close to three hours after arriving, it is almost time for Faulkner and his team to play.

* * *

In the makeshift locker room, Faulkner provides his last-minute talk before the team tips off. The team has stretched and the women have

Figure 3.4. Faulkner diagramming a play during the Clayton State game. (Photo taken by author.)

lost. He steps up to the large dry-erase board and scribbles down the defensive assignments: who is defending whom.

The team circles up, fists extended toward the center. "Our Father, who art in Heaven," they intone in unison. Finishing the Lord's Prayer, they break and head to the court. The first few minutes are a frenzy of back-and-forth possessions. Neither team secures much of a lead until UNG stretches out to a nine-point lead about midway through the first half. With Williams on the bench with two fouls, Clayton State slowly gnaws away at UNG's lead and ties the game with less than six minutes to go in the first half.

During the media time-out, Faulkner lights into his players. He is down on one knee, a dry-erase clipboard in one hand and a black marker in the other. He yells above the music blasting from the arena's speakers: "Listen, listen, hey guys remember, the last three games we closed the half very, very poorly."

Faulkner's hand clings the marker, his forehead reddening: "We have to close strong right here! We have to close strong! We have to have effort!" His voice softens again. "We got a time-out left that we will use this half. Play as hard as you can. I will give us a time-out. Play as hard as you can right here." Then the yelling again, the clinched hand, the red forehead: "I don't think we are running the floor and running our transitions as hard as we can. Every-freakin'-body we got is jogging their ass up and down the floor. Turn and sprint and get to your lane and let's go set the dribble drag into five out and let's move the basketball."

The team fails to respond to Faulkner's demand. They find themselves down by two going into halftime.

I follow the team into the locker room. The players seem ragged. This is their fourth game in the past week, and they are tired. No one talks. After several minutes of quiet and no coaches in the room, I leave and head down the hallway. I see all five coaches hunched over sheets of paper. Faulkner is pacing and reading. All are looking at the first-half stats. No one speaks. Finally, Faulkner says "Okay" and he leads the coaches into the locker room. I follow again, this time a little uncomfortably. Eating chicken parmesan at Rocky's two hours before a game with the coach is one thing; following him into his locker room in the middle of a game and with his team losing is another. I feel as if I am trespassing. I know I would be a bit uncomfortable with an outsider sitting in on my class immediately after my students performed poorly and exhibited a lack of effort. I know I would be uncomfortable with someone sitting in while I expressed my disappointment and pushed for stronger performance. The locker room is Faulkner's classroom and the players are his pupils. I don't want to impose on his work anymore than I would want him to impose on mine. I also don't want to take up space. The locker room is small, even smaller with twelve (tall, big) players, four assistant coaches, one student-manager, and a livid head coach. I demurely stand outside the door, behind Brian, the six-feet-nine-inch graduate assistant. But I can still hear Faulkner.

With his suit jacket off and a green dry-erase marker in his hand, Faulkner teaches. He is just shouting while teaching.

* * *

Thirty seconds into the second half, Clayton State pushes the lead to six before UNG ties it at fifty-one. Clayton State is out-muscling UNG. Faulkner mentioned Clayton State's athleticism during the pre-game talk, and his players needed to get bodies on them and fight for rebounds. In their loss to Clayton State last season, UNG gave up stunning sixteen offensive rebounds. During the media time-out, Faulkner is steaming. It is the angriest I have seen him all season. "Look guys, now listen. We have got to get some freakin' rebounds. They are kicking our butts down there and we are not manning up. T. J. [Williams]: you are the baddest dude out here. Now go show them."

He quickly calms and begins drawing on the clipboard with his black marker.

"Let's stay box defense for one possession. Let's stay box down here and then let's go, uh, let's go Up Elbow. Let's go Up Elbow down here."

Brennan speaks up. He points to Faulkner's board while talking. "Hey, when they check our ball screen right here I got to come up and help . . ."

Faulkner listens but the media time-out is short. He interrupts and builds on Brennan's suggestion. "Hey, listen, no, even better. Ebo [Smith], you are right here. When you got a ball screen, go under it. Don't go over the thing. Get under it."

The horn blasts signaling the end of the time-out, and the team rushes back onto the court as Faulkner slings the board against the chairs on the bench. Hawkins picks it up, erases it, and slides it under his chair.

The game—and, eventually, the rest of the season—turns at the 6:39 mark. The fingers of a Clayton State shooter accidentally catch Tanner Plemmons in the left eye. Plemmons, a starting guard for the Nighthawks, goes to one knee rubbing his eye. Plemmons is currently leading the team in points. Faulkner sends in a sub for Plemmons and Plemmons makes his way to the head trainer, Matt Daniel. Plemmons's eye is bloodshot, and he rapidly blinks. The head trainer works on Plemmons. He administers eyewash and tests his vision. In the background, the game continues with Clayton State gaining a six-point lead. Plemmons and the head trainer leave the bench and head behind the bleachers. Daniel administers more eye tests.

At the four-minute media time-out, Faulkner is much more composed than before even though his team is down, his best player, Plemmons, is out, and his second-best player, Brennan, is battling flu-like symptoms. He sketches a quick play: "Hey, listen. Right here we are going to go Zip 3 for Shaq [Cantrell]. Let's don't give them an illegal screen. Shaq, I want that about right here. So, Corey [Green], go a little bit early to let that initial screen go high. Sean's got the ball here [and] Ebo's in the corner and then run up this side right there. And Sean, you gotta be careful about that guy jumping right here."

Green speaks up. Like Brennan, he points to Faulkner's board. "Wait for the screen and step inside, all right?"

With 25.2 seconds left in the game, Clayton State is up 85–82. Faulkner calls a time-out and draws up a play. He draws Up 2, which has Smith run off a flair screen for an open three-point shot. If the shot is not open, Smith will pass the ball down low to Cantrell. The play looks effective. Smith is one of the better shooters on the team and hit a shot earlier in the week against Young Harris College to tie the game late. Unfortunately, plays on paper and plays executed on the court are different. As with football, points and wins are not tallied for effective plays but for the effective embodiment of plays. The rhetorical situation, particularly the context and constraints, surrounding the delivery of this text is much different from the rhetorical situation surrounding the delivery of this play in the gym back in Dahlonega. The players are tired. It is late in the game. They are without one of their better players and are being out-muscled. They have run similar plays, so Clayton State may know what is coming next. Many UNG players are playing in this gym for the first time. Each gym floor feels different. Each goal and net look a little different. All these constraints weigh on the play—some positive, some negative—and when the team runs onto the court during the last 25.2 seconds, Green turns the ball over within fourteen seconds. Smith never touches the ball.

UNG loses by two.

Back in the locker room, Faulkner addresses his players. Most players have stripped off their jerseys and piled them into the middle of the floor. Remnants of ankle tape and balled-up socks are strewn around. Some players are wrapped in towels. Others sit in just their shorts. Faulkner breaks the thick silence:

> Guys, I still think we got a chance to get really, really good. You just got to not let losing one game turn into losing two, three, four, five games in a row or something like that. Okay? Let's make sure we stay together and that's what I love about you guys. . . . Now, I also want you to understand this: we played like crap at times. Okay? For more than probably half of the game, I don't think we played real well . . . walk out of here disgusted but you better not walk out of here discouraged about anything. Disgusted with how we played, disappointed with how we lost, but you better not walk out of here discouraged with where we are as a basketball team. There's ton of basketball left to play this season, okay?

The team groups up: "Our Father, who art in Heaven . . ."

* * *

On the way home, we stop at Rocky's to pick up our preordered sandwiches. Daniel, the head trainer, is on the phone trying to reach an ophthalmologist. Later, I learn Plemmons's retina was partially detached. He undergoes successful surgery two days later and is out for the season. I also learn Brennan, the guard who spoke up during the media time-out and notched the second-most points on the team against Clayton State, has the flu. Faulkner's two best guards are now sidelined. To navigate the challenging upcoming games, Faulkner will get his players back in the gym on Monday and do what he has done for twelve years: teach.

The bus is quiet on the way home. The only noise is the eating of sandwiches.

PRACTICE
JANUARY 22ND, 2015

Following their loss to Clayton State, the Nighthawks drop their next three out of four games to sit at 12–5 overall and 6–4 in conference play. Plemmons is also out for the rest of the season. Reacting to the losing skid, Plemmons's season-ending injury, and the schedule that has his team playing against an opponent for a second time, Faulkner introduces a new play called *LA*, so named because, according to Brennan, it "is like old Shaq and Kobe," who won three straight NBA championships with the Los Angeles Lakers in the early 2000s. As Brennan says, LA is "mainly for the three, four, and five guys to stay in the middle of the floor and get their defenders moving so their defenders don't just sit in the paint waiting on the guards to attack." With an offensive philosophy of stretching the floor and opening up shots for the guards, LA is, in Faulkner's words, "kinda 180 from what we generally try to do." Yet, Faulkner stresses, "we're not totally changing our philosophy, but it is a change of pace so to speak. Like I said, if it is a football team that runs all the time, you put in a pass play and hopefully you catch somebody off guard."

Faulkner does not rely on traditional text to teach new plays. Instead, he breaks down the complexity of a play into manageable portions, which players run in practice without a defense. One of the more common exercises is three on zero. Three offensive players race down the court with a ball and run through portions of a play without defenders. Then two additional players are added to make it five on zero. With this approach, Faulkner looks to "take bits and pieces of what we are trying to do and break it down in parts. Then put it back together into a five on zero and then incorporate the type of movement and then go ahead and do five on five." Such a tactile learning experience meets the needs of his players because, as I quoted in the epigraph to this chapter, Faulkner believes "guys learn a lot better [this way]. The most athletic guys learn by doing. They don't learn by looking at it in a playbook or looking at it drawn up on a whiteboard." Faulkner later retracts his statement a bit when he talks of drawing plays on the board during a film session. He describes such an approach as "draw it up and transfer it to the floor and hope it resonates with them." Yet the emphasis comes back to running the play during

practice over analyzing the play on a whiteboard. When I asked Core if
not having a playbook like in football hinders performance, Core didn't
think so. He explained, "I think 90 percent of [my teammates] are visual
learners and kinesthetic learners, so they need to put their bodies in those
positions. It's what's going to help them learn the best."

Core explains further how the coaches teach a new play:

> The first thing that I notice that they do is they put us in a drill, and they
> don't tell us we are running a new play. They put us in a drill and they
> tell us that "okay, your job is to go screen this guy and you pop open over
> here" for example. Then after that they say, "Okay, we spent all this time
> running this drill now it's a play." And they say, "This is what you are look-
> ing for." And I think it is to prevent us from being so robotic. Put us in like
> a little breakdown drill where there is only three people on the court. So
> that way they know you can read off of this and then when we say, "Okay,
> this is a play." Then it lets you play with more freedom.

To teach this new play LA, Faulkner, in Drew's words, "gave us the
meat and threw on the sides later."

> 'Cause it is a triangle-based offense, so we ran three on three working on
> just the triangle screen down, screen across, screen across, and then down.
> Just the movement within those three because those three don't move out
> of that position. He didn't even tell us [we were running a new play]. It
> was just a drill before it was three on three. . . . And then the next thing
> right after that it was "Here's the play. We just ran it for fifteen minutes
> playing defense and everything. Here's the other two parts to it. Here's
> what the other two people are doing, and this is a play we are going to run.
> And this is how we get into it" and stuff like that. So he gave us the meat
> and threw the sides on later kinda deal.

With LA logged in the player's mental rolodex of plays, the team
prepares for a weekend road game against Montevallo, one of the best
teams in the conference. There are fewer than nine games left in the
season. UNG sits in fourth place in the western division of the conference. Montevallo is tied for first. UNG loses by fourteen.

YOUNG HARRIS COLLEGE HOME GAME
FEBRUARY 4TH, 2015

It's Spirit Night. Students are decked out in extravagant amalgamations
of blue, white, and yellow—the school colors. One student is feath-
ered—literally—another is wearing a tutu, another is dressed as a king
complete with a regal robe and hat. Inside the gym, students separate
into their Greek affiliations: Kappa Delta and Delta Zeta at opposite
ends, Pi Kappa Alpha and Kappa Sigma at opposite ends.

Rival Young Harris College is in town for a game billed as the Battle for Blood Mountain in reference to the highest point in Georgia and a peak geographically separating the two schools. The private Methodist-affiliated Young Harris is located just an hour north of Dahlonega and, within the UNG athletics department, is spoken of with equal levels of disdain and admiration. It's a private school with extra funds to direct toward athletics and scholarships. It's a school with a $100 million endowment for a student population of just over one thousand five hundred compared to UNG's $52 million endowment for nineteen thousand students spread across five campuses. It's a school with a former Georgia secretary of state as the president.

Earlier in the season, UNG beat Young Harris at the buzzer when Brennan hit an improbable and improvised jumper. Though Young Harris has a poor record (entering the contest, they were 8–12, 2–10 in the conference), Young Harris's athleticism and tenacious defense has given UNG trouble in the past.

I'm pacing the bottom floor of the gym where the coaches' offices, locker room, and training rooms are located. Above me, the women's game has entered halftime, and I feel the steady thud of the pep band's brass and bass sections. I peek into Faulkner's office. He is dressed in a light-blue shirt, pale yellow tie, and gray suit. The color pattern nicely complements his light complexion. His jacket is hanging over his chair, and he is shuffling paperwork. Halftime of the women's game is almost over, and two women on the Young Harris team frantically pour out of their locker room. "Where is another door to the gym?" they ask quickly, "We've been locked out." Their eyes dart back and forth; they are eager to join their team. Matt Daniel, the head trainer, points the way and then runs alongside them to help them navigate the serpentine hallways beneath the gym.

Referees for the men's game walk in, dressed in black and pulling black suitcases on wheels. Travis ushers them to their own locker room. Hawkins sees an assistant coach for Young Harris and greets him cheerfully. "Jesus, you look good," Hawkins says ebulliently, bear-hugging the assistant coach. A videographer shooting a promotion for the Admissions Office makes his way down the corridor. Twelve more long minutes before the women's game ends. Players, coaches, refs, and trainers make forced but pleasant conversation with each other.

Then it's time for the first of two talks by Faulkner before tipoff. I follow him into the locker room for the first time, and the pungent smell hits me. The locker room is divided into two rooms. The first has two leather sofas perpendicularly arranged against the walls. A large UNG rug stretches across the floor. Against the third wall is a dry-erase board. Markers, erasers, a television remote, a slim Gideon's Bible, and a placard reading "There's No Ceiling on Effort" sit on the shelf. A forty-three-inch Vizio television hangs in the corner. The second room is the locker room proper: lockers, bathroom, and shower.

Faulkner gathers his players. It is a tight fit for thirteen players, four coaches, a student manager, and myself. On the floor, Brennan is using a foam roller to loosen his leg muscles. Williams is the only player not wearing the blue-and-white long-sleeved camouflage shooting shirt. Faulkner stresses the need for communication between teammates when defending against the screens and not giving up many points in transition to Young Harris: "All screening action: make sure you are doing a good job talking and communicating. I think a huge key to this game is not allowing them points in transition and not allowing them to get going in transition. They kinda thrive on that."

When emphasizing specific defense plans, he resorts back to granting players autonomy: "So everybody has got to really, really sprint back and remember in transition you don't guard a man, per se. Okay? You get back and we start talking and get matched up however we can. So in other words, if you are guarding 3, you don't always have to match up with 3 in transition. We got to get back and talk and know what we are doing."

Faulkner uncaps the blue marker and turns to draw on the board. He mentions some defensive plays they will run in the game and spends time visually representing one of the more complex plays Young Harris runs: "We'll go half court fist, we'll go double fist, we'll go box some. We will do some of our pressing stuff. Remember if we go to box, what we've talked about today [during the early-afternoon shootaround], when that ball gets here and we got this back line here back here when it hits right there, remember this guy we're kinda closing."

Faulkner is pointing to specific movements he has drawn on the board: "This guy is coming to trap it, and this off-sides guy, we gotta come down on this guy. Remember we talked about that. [Green, Cantrell, Varrichione] could be you at the four; [Lawrence] it could be you at the four some. So know what we are doing with that right there."

Offensively, Faulkner stresses the need to move the basketball and to stay wide in hopes of finding an open shot or opening lanes to the basket. He ends his four-minute talk by imploring his team to keep up "positive energy for forty minutes. Very, very positive, a lot of energy the whole time."

After warming up on the court, the team convenes for the final talk before the opening tip. Faulkner only talks for forty-five seconds. In blue marker, he writes the starters' names on the board and the number of the man each will be defending. A final comment from Faulkner before the team huddles: "Anytime we go double fist [a defensive alignment], understand match-ups could get messed around. And you got the freedom to switch and get back however you want to anytime when we are doing that. Be ready to change and throw a bunch of different defenses at them." The team huddles: "Our Father, who art in Heaven . . ."

I follow behind the coaches down the hallway and up the stairs. The players have already rushed onto the court. I am behind Faulkner. I wait for him to go through the door and onto the court and he turns and ushers me in first. "You nervous?" I ask, patting him on the shoulder. A big grin breaks out on his face. "How can you tell?" he asks. He then adds, "A little." I smile and we walk out into the chaos of Spirit Night.

The score shows a close game, but UNG seems slow. They are not playing with the positive energy Faulkner asked for. Young Harris is getting easy points and steals, both of which Faulkner addressed earlier in the locker room. The band and crowd noise is too loud for me to hear Faulkner address his team during the mandatory media time-outs. I lean in hoping to catch his voice on my recorder but cannot. I wonder if the players, who are less than a foot closer than I am, can hear him.

UNG leads by one point midway through the first half. It will be their last lead of the game. Young Harris takes control and hits a three pointer while the horn sounds to end the first half. Again, I find myself in a locker room with a frustrated team and an even more frustrated coach. The players are in the locker room proper. I am sitting on the sofa. Outside the door, I can hear assistant-coach Josh Travis yelling at someone in the hallway.

Faulkner walks into the locker room with an eerie calm. He talks for almost seven minutes and oscillates wildly between calm and furious. He starts by calmly asking how the man hit a three pointer as time expired. Core, who was guarding the man, explains what happened, and Faulkner and Core have a brief exchange. Then Faulkner quickly turns frustrated.

> We are just kinda standing there like "Coach called box [a defensive alignment], we can take a little break now and we don't have to guard." What did I tell ya? What'd I tell ya yesterday, and what'd I tell ya today? Perimeter guys, what did I tell ya? It's a freakin challenge, and we backed away from it! Because this cat is lighting our asses up. Tyler's man [number] 5 is doing whatever he wants and you are just saying "Okay, that's fine." We are just soft. We don't want to take the challenge and say "I am fixing to guard this guy's butt." Plain and simple. We want to back away. I don't understand that. I don't understand why we don't have enough guts to go out there and say "I'm going to stop his ass." . . . Do we care? It

certainly doesn't look like we care by what we are doing. They played five guys thirty-eight minutes a game, and they are running by you like you are standing still. How does that happen? Do you care about it anymore? Does anybody care about it? Don't answer me. Fuckin' show me when we get up there.

He eases off after a minute and talks more specifically about defensive alignments. He then asks the players what else they saw. Lawrence says, "We just gotta talk."

The second half continues the way of the first. Young Harris makes a quick basket, and following a missed layup by Williams and a turnover by Smith, Young Harris hits another shot to go up by eleven. UNG cuts the lead to four but the lead balloons back up to eleven points in five minutes. Young Harris wins by five. Again, I wait uncomfortably in the locker room following a poor performance by the team. Rather than ripping into his team's poor effort, Faulkner comes across conciliatory and positive: "I believe we are going to come in here on Saturday and beat these guys. We are going to practice tomorrow at two [p.m.]. It is going to be very light. This is as flat as I have seen this group all year, energy-wise. But if we come and play with energy Saturday, and I believe we are going to, we win the basketball game."

Again, the huddle. Again, the Lord's Prayer.

On Saturday, they beat Montevallo, the top team in the conference and a team that beat them by fourteen points ten days earlier.

PRACTICE
FEBRUARY 24TH, 2015

Snow fell last night. While students make snowballs, snowmen, and snow angels, the men's basketball is having what could be their last practice of the season. Tomorrow, they play Georgia Southwestern. Two weeks earlier, Georgia Southwestern handed them their worst loss of the season: a twenty-point battering. If the Nighthawks win, their season is prolonged and they make the conference tournament. If not, the season will be over. Core's college career will be over. So will Lawrence's. Despite the pressure, the team looks relaxed, almost carefree.

GEORGIA SOUTHWESTERN HOME GAME
FEBRUARY 25TH, 2015

The night of the game, Georgia's governor declares a state of emergency as a winter storm is again moving into the north-Georgia region. Sitting at home with the wind whirling and the ice accumulating outside, I stream the game.

UNG loses.

The season is over. They finish with a 15–11 overall record and 9–10 in conference play. At the beginning of the season, Peach Belt Conference coaches picked the Nighthawks to finish eighth. The coaches-turned-prognosticators were close; UNG ties rival Young Harris for seventh place.

THE WRITING PRACTICES OF COLLEGE BASKETBALL

When I arranged to follow the basketball team for one season, I carried certain expectations for the kinds and uses of text I would witness. My experience working with first-year football players at Auburn framed these expectations. For football, physical text is vital. While the NFL has proudly partnered with Microsoft and endorses Surface tablets, many professional players and coaches still prefer physical text. Physical playbooks are central to the writing practices of football. During games, coaches prowl the sidelines, gripping sheets of paper. The television camera catches a coach stuffing paper into his waistband, freeing his hands to motion to his players. Coaches use paper to cover their mouths as they shout directions to their players or speak through headsets to coaches sitting high above the stadium.

Yet as I moved through basketball practices, rode on the bus, sat on the bench and in the coaches' offices, the lack of interaction between people and physical text surprised me. Reflecting on how basketball players learn plays, then, I start with what they do not do. They do not learn plays by engaging with physically scripted plays. When they see visual representations of plays—drawn only by Faulkner from my observations—these visual representations are reminders of what they should do. Their bodies already know the plays; Faulkner is simply visually representing the plays as a way to talk about what they are planning to do.

Faulkner mentioned to me that the athletics department has a license with a software company called FastDraw, a platform for basketball coaches to draw and disseminate plays digitally. Because it's popular with Division I and NBA coaches, I was surprised none of the players had heard of FastDraw or had even seen the website. Fourth-year senior Travis Core, who has been with the team the longest, seemed slightly disappointed Faulkner never introduced his players to it. Except for hooking up an Xbox 360 to a dated RCA projector television to watch game film, the team has no direct engagement with any digital resources to learn or reflect on plays. The team also does not have a physical playbook. T. J. Williams was the only player I talked with who had a physical playbook in high school. All the others dismissed the need for a playbook at the high-school and college level. Faulkner did tell me he has all the plays written out, but none of his players has seen this list. Faulkner says he would like to diagram them all—like Brennan did with the play Ear—but, according to him, "it's a time issue." With a small staff, coaches devote time to teaching plays, not diagramming them for future use.

Faulkner doesn't patrol the sideline with a thick list of plays and is not shuffling through paper during practices. Nor does his coaching staff. Moreover, Faulkner admitted to me with a slight laugh that he hardly looks at the stats his coaching staff charts during a game. During halftime and at the end of the game, people at the scoring table print out stats, which they hand to coaches on both teams. Faulkner pours over these stats before addressing his team. At home and in his office, he takes notes on his iPhone when reviewing game film. He keeps copious notes on loose sheets of paper organized in manila file folders and labeled with the opposition's names. When I flipped through Faulkner's Columbus State and Georgia Southwestern file folders, I got the sense Faulkner haphazardly keeps all his notes. He composes some on green paper, some on yellow legal paper, some on printer paper. He files diagrammed plays, lineups, and film breakdowns—minute-by-minute analyses of game films. Figure 3.5 represents Faulkner's thoughts on how to improve against Columbus State, particularly how to play against Columbus State's defensive formation called *amoeba zone.*

Physical text grounds Faulkner's reflection in figure 3.5. However, Faulkner and his staff teach plays, and players learn plays, with little to no direct interaction with scripted text. Here is an extracurricular writing practice in which physical or digital text is absent in the learning process. Players are learning text without text. This point may strike a reader as odd when juxtaposed with chapter 2, which provides detailing readings of scripted plays. To be sure, a traditional digitally or physically compiled playbook is more common in football than in basketball. But the absence of a compiled playbook in basketball does not mean plays are unimportant. In chapter 2, I argue plays are multimodal, dialectically constructed between players and coaches, historically situated to the needs of the immediate audience and context, and anticipative of bodily enactment—like lines in a screenplay or notes in a musical score, they are written to be performed. In addition, I answer the query *what do plays do?* by suggesting plays *do* competitive bodily action. To make this paired argument, I walked through several physically and digitally

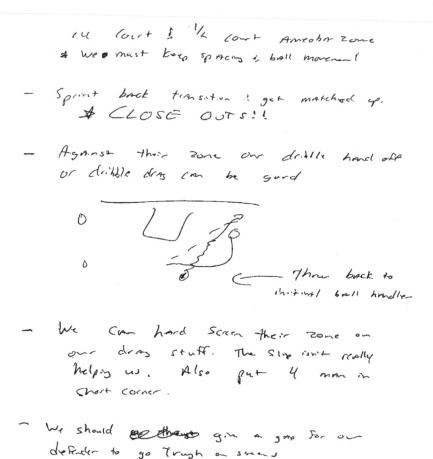

Figure 3.5. Handwritten notes by Faulkner composed as he watched tape of the game against Columbus State. I use a forward slash to delineate between the sections on the report. The report reads as follows: "1/4 court & ½ court amoeba zone & we must keep spacing & ball movement / Sprint back transition & get matched up. CLOSE OUTS!! / Against their zone our dribble hand off or dribble drag can be good / throw back to initial ball handler / We can hard screen their zone on our drag stuff. The slip isn't really helping us. Also put 4 man in short corner / We should give a gap for our defender to go through on screen."

scripted plays. I continue this argument in this chapter about plays, but, as one helpful early reader pointed out, playbooks are absent for the UNG team, and scripted plays only minimally appear. So are scripted plays important or not to the writing practices of our student-athletes?

This question places more importance on the text than on the cognitive process student-athletes leverage to engage with the text. No matter whether the student-athlete spends free time idly scrolling through his team's playbook uploaded on an iPad or has never seen all the team's plays compiled into a single document, the student-athlete is using the same cognitive processes to learn and embody the play. Certainly, it's fun to ponder the reasons football and not basketball rely more strongly on scripted plays and a compiled playbook. It may be because basketball is more free flowing and rapid; players have thirty-five seconds to take a shot and only have to coordinate meaning among five teammates, with a whole team often including only ten total players. Football is slower. Teams can huddle and ponder for thirty-five seconds before even snapping the ball. Once the play is complete, the teams stop, ponder, and wait again. And they have to coordinate meaning among eleven players on the field and the many coaches on the sidelines and up high in the press boxes. Regardless, I place the emphasis on how players learn the plays. No matter whether the play is shouted from midcourt by a coach or drawn carefully on a whiteboard during spring football practice, student-athletes rely on three central cognitive processes.

HOW PLAYERS LEARN PLAYS

UNG players learn plays through three cognitive processes that emphasize bodily learning:

- spatial orientation
- haptic communication
- scaffolded situations

Though I delineate among the three, such delineation is rather artificial. When learning plays, all three processes coalesce.

Learning through Spatial Orientation

Composition studies research productively nests location with the act of writing and gravitates toward in situ studies of writers writing because, as Nedra Reynolds (2004) argues, the "*where* of writing" (176) affects the how and what of writing. For composition studies, Reynolds's where of writing has long been first-year composition, which is understandable, as the discipline grew out of the classroom and not the other way around. Yet, as Kathleen Blake Yancey (2014) writes in her editor's introduction to a two-issue special issue of *College Composition and Communication* on locations of writing, "Our discipline's historical focus on a single site of writing—that of first-year composition in the United States—has expanded and diversified" (214). We follow the writer to writing,

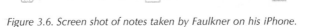

●●●○○ AT&T 📶   11:11 AM   ⊕ ✳ 84% ▰▱

< Back

March 2, 2015, 8:24 AM

Motion Offense

Think about a few simple
concepts for how we can teach
motion offense.
• penetrate and play off two feet
    When penetrator jump stops
have other guys cut off him

• make ball go side to side. Stop
driving back in to where others
are.

Do we want to look at cutter
screener system?

Look at having guys screen in
"pairs". This way one guy has

🗑   ⬆   ✎

Figure 3.6. Screen shot of notes taken by Faulkner on his iPhone.

whenever and wherever. Location, Reynolds's "*where* of writing," is vital
to how UNG players engage with and use text for their sport. The players I studied understood location as their spatial relationships to others
(i.e., teammates and opponents) and areas on the court. When I asked
players in my office to draw and explicate plays, all started by graphically representing the basketball court. Although some added additional
details—such as out-of-bounds lines and half-court lines—all included
a circle for the basket and a semicircle for the three-point line (see
fig. 3.7). Before graphically representing themselves, their teammates,
the opponent, or physical movements, such as passes and screens, all
spatially represented the play's location. Faulkner did the same. The
whiteboard he scribbles on during time-outs in a game has the black
outlines of a full court imposed on it (see fig. 3.2, for example). When
Faulkner sketched formations and plays, he began with the basket and
three-point line. He went the additional step of adding the key (i.e., the
shaded rectangle area extending from beneath the basket) but no other

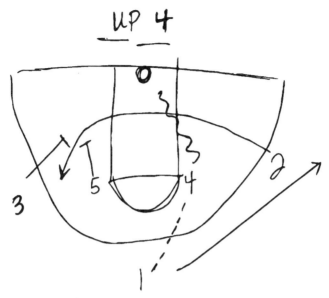

Figure 3.7. Sophomore forward T. J. Williams's drawing of the offensive play UP 4.

details, like the out-of-bounds lines. No matter his level of frustration, he always began with spatially orienting himself and his players to the court when visually representing a play. The players' movements and locations are intertwined. For players to understand a play and for Faulkner or any of the assistant coaches to teach a play, the players and the coaches must first begin with the location of the play's enactment.

Location also figures into how players and coaches brainstorm and develop plays. I started this chapter with insight into Faulkner's teaching as seen in an early-November practice. Faulkner adjusted a particular play based on watching a play unfold and then receiving player feedback. He moved Cantrell around slightly and pointed out a wrinkle in the play he had been considering but wasn't ready to decide on until he saw the play in action. Core spoke up and suggested the same wrinkle might apply to a different play. Faulkner agreed and made the change. When Faulkner saw how the play unfolded on the court, he knew he wanted to make a change. It wasn't enough for him to run through the play in his head or even on a sheet of paper; he needed to see how the play spatially operated. In addition, Faulkner added a new play midway through the season. As he told me, watching how teams defended UNG provided an impetus for LA. Because Faulkner wants to spread the floor and get open shots for his guards, the opposing big men were either creeping away from the basket and toward defending the guards or waiting by the basket for the guards to attack. In other words, the defensive big men were not concerned with UNG's offensive big men. As a counter, Faulkner designed LA to get UNG's big men more involved in the offense and, hopefully, open driving lanes and shots for the guards. The play's exigence comes from watching how opponents spatially orient themselves on the court. Location factors into invention when the team looks to develop a new play or add a wrinkle to an existing one. Finally, through emphasizing location during writing, the student-athletes I studied oriented themselves in relation to their teammates and opponents.

Before the Young Harris game, Faulkner stressed that Young Harris would run a one-three-one zone in which the five defenders do not guard specific players but guard areas on the court. Faulkner reminded his team of plays effective against a zone and those effective against a man to man. The text the players inscribe on the court, the play they run, is a direct reflection of how the defense spatially arranges itself. In addition, the spatial arrangement of teammates can help players remember and then implement the signaled play. When I talked with Williams, I asked him whether he ever forgets a play during a game. He responded, "I feel like that happens sometimes because like when [another player] moves, you know that the spot that they just moved from is where you are supposed to be or in the general area. Like if someone is near me I will be like 'Oh, crap, I gotta set a screen for them.' I feel like that happens sometimes. Because the speed of the game sometimes you might call something and be like 'uh' and taking a minute and then you go right into it." One of Williams's jobs is setting screens for guards. If he forgets a play, he looks to those around him. If a guard is near him then, in his words, "I gotta set a screen for them."

When I handed Lawrence the play Brennan drew, Lawrence held it and looked lost. I asked him if he recognized the play. He said no. During the course of our interview, Lawrence kept picking up the play. He seemed frustrated that as a senior on the team he didn't recognize it. When our interview concluded, Lawrence returned to the play, again unprompted by me. He said he remembers most of the plays by "where we are trying to get the ball to." This "to" could be a location on the court or a physical player—though the "to" makes me think it's the former. Either way, Lawrence knows plays in relation to others and in relation to areas on the court. Lawrence's basketball literacy and the literacy of the entire team hinges on spatial relationships. Players interact with these relationships; they bounce off them, screen them, push against them. Players' writing practices entail learning through feel, specifically haptic communication.

Learning through Haptic Communication

Laura Micciche (2014) draws attention to "relational matters . . . as writing essentials" (497) in her work on material rhetorics. Informed by postprocess theory, Micciche explores "writing's withness" (495) through adaptive and collaborative dimensions of writing. She asserts that "to think of writing as a practice of coexistence is to imagine a *merging of various forms of matter . . .* in an activity not solely dependent on one's control but made possible by elements that codetermine writing's possibility" (498; emphasis added). I emphasize the phrase "merging of various forms of matter" to illustrate the connection between Micciche's position on material rhetoric and what the thirteen players on UNG's basketball team do when they learn plays and write these plays through their bodies. The learning of plays necessitates Micciche's withness. The players learn plays in coordination with others, a process I refer to as *haptic communication.* This term attends to the physical interaction between players and between players and coaches during the learning process. Haptic communication is a prominent sensory rhetoric for student-athletes in general. Most players learn through touch. And like orienting oneself in relation to another body, haptic communication shows how learning a basketball play is a thoroughly bodily learning experience.

During practices, Faulkner grabs a player by the elbow, moving him around and through a space. Assistant coach Simmons, with his experience of working with post players, puts his hands on a player's hips and begins twisting them into the desired position. Teammates do the same. They jostle a teammate into the needed position to run the play. Similar to psychologist Mihaly Csikszentmihalyi's (1998) concept of flow, players across all sports and across all levels often talk about getting a feel for the game and knowing through the body how a game is unfolding. Yet student-athletes' talk of flow often dwindles into the metaphysical in the sense that they are not talking about something concrete but about something almost ethereal, incalculable, and impossible to teach: how does a coach teach a player to get a *feel* for the game? Haptic communication is the concrete representation of getting a feel for the game. For the UNG basketball players, the learning of plays necessitates touch on the part of each other and the coaches.

For example, a prominent role for Williams is setting screens for Brennan, Core, Smith, and the other guards. A screen is a common basketball maneuver designed to separate an offensive player from his defender. Typically set by the center or forward, the screener positions his body close to his teammate with the ball. The teammate with the ball dribbles toward the screener attempting to run his defender into the screener and create enough separation between himself and his defender to shoot the ball or dribble toward the basket. When setting a screen, Williams feels where his man is and positions his body accordingly. Reading where Williams has positioned himself, Brennan moves toward the screen (again, returning to spatial location) and runs his defender into Williams's screen. Williams feels the impact, blocks Brennan's defender just for a slice of a second, and then pushes away, pivoting his body away from Brennan's defender and away from his own defender, looking to either receive the ball from Brennan or move toward setting a different screen. Watching Williams in a game is like watching a pinball collide against pads and flippers; he smashes against defenders and, following the collision, seeks the next target. As Williams says when he forgets a play, "If someone is near me I will be like 'Oh, crap, I gotta set a screen for them.'" After working through spatial orientation in his learning process, his next step is haptic communication, and he connects his body with another. As Faulkner says, "The most athletic guys learn by doing. They don't learn by looking at it in a playbook or looking at it drawn up on a whiteboard."

Learning through Scaffolded Situations

When Drew says "he [Faulkner] gave us the meat and threw the sides on later kinda deal," he is describing the learning concept of scaffolding. Isabelle Thompson (2009) tailors the general pedagogical process of scaffolding to writing center theory and practice. According to Thompson, scaffolding is connected with Lev Vygotsky's (1978) views of cognitive development popularized through Jerome Bruner's (1978) research. Scaffolding is just as the metaphor suggests: leading learners to higher levels of learning through the process of building sequential knowledge in increasingly more challenging steps. Thompson contends the ultimate goal is helping students "learn how to regulate their own learning and performance" (Thompson 2009, 422). Thompson draws on the coauthored work of Sadhana Puntambekar and Roland Hübscher in delineating four features of scaffolding: intersubjectivity, ongoing diagnosis, dialogic and interactive, and fading (Puntambekar and Hübscher 2005, 2–3). These four features lead toward greater agency on the part of the learner. Intersubjectivity focuses on joint ownership between novice and expert (*writer* and *tutor* in Thompson's article and *player* and *coach* in this chapter). In ongoing diagnosis, the coach assesses the cognitive challenge facing the player and juxtaposes this challenge with the player's current skill level. The coach then draws the player into practicing the new skill during the dialogic and interactive feature of scaffolding before fading in the fourth feature and allowing the player to regulate their own learning.

Faulkner and his coaching staff rely on scaffolding to break down complex plays into manageable cognitive and physical moves. One activity asks players to run through an offensive play without any defenders. The majority of the practices I observed started with three players racing down the court without defenders, rapidly passing and cutting before taking a shot. As Faulkner says, "We try to do breakdown drills where we break [the play] down on a three on zero type of situation where we can take bits and pieces of what we are trying to do and break it down in parts and then put it back together into a five on zero."

Core told me that many times the players are not aware they are learning a new play when they are running the three on zero or five on zero drills: "The first thing that I notice that they [coaches] do is they put us in a drill, and they don't tell us we are running a new play. They put us in a drill and they tell us, 'Okay, your job is to screen this guy and pop open over here,' for example. Then after that they say, 'Okay, we spent all this time running this drill. Now it's a play.'"

The three on zero or five on zero drills, Core says, are a "way they [coaches] know you can read off of this and then they, 'Okay, this is a play,' then it lets you play with more freedom." In his response, Travis emphasizes spatial location to learning a play—"pop open over here"—and connects with the larger goal Faulkner has for the offense: manipulating plays and freelancing plays. Faulkner wants his players to understand how plays work but not stick to a play to the team's detriment. Core's repeatedly stated point that coaches do not want players to be "robotic" struck me during our conversation. Core even said Faulkner gets frustrated when players follow a play too closely: "I know he [Faulkner] yells at us sometimes for running the play robotically." Core continues and mimics Faulkner's voice and demeanor, "Like, you know, 'we run the plays to get you guys open. If you are open doing it a little differently, do it.'" By breaking plays into segments and little breakdown drills, Faulkner ensures his players understand how plays operate, which provides them with the freedom to improvise, what Faulkner calls the "freelance type of thing," within a game situation. Core refers to this freelance type of thing when he says players need to "read off of this," the "this" referring to specific individual movements within a larger play. In addition, returning to Thompson's (2009) discussion of scaffolding and the larger goal of scaffolding, Core is speaking of regulating his own learning and performance. Faulkner wants his players to transfer their knowledge of one play to their understanding of another play. He wants them to work within the constructs of a play and not feel chained to what the play dictates. In sum, he wants his players to regulate their own performance within his construct.

Faulkner adds a defense once players understand how the collective movements within the play contribute to the whole. Lawrence says it is as simple as "just throw the defense out there and just start working." Brennan speaks in even simpler terms: "Then you would go out and do it. Just repetition." But once defenders are on the court, Faulkner tries to create a game-like situation—five on five. Now there are ten players on the court. All ten players are locating themselves on the court and in relation to each other. All ten players focus on watching how their specific movements within a play scaffold toward the complexity of the larger play.

* * *

By way of ending, I turn to my first conversation with Faulkner. In the past, I have met resistance from within athletics departments because I position myself as an academic interested in writing about college-sports literacy. All too often, professors and athletics departments don't communicate well—each leery of the other. When I approach athletics department administration, I feel the need to establish my ethos quickly, show I am not interesting in chasing celebrity student-athletes (a *jersey chaser*, as some are called) or sketching yet another a screed on college sports. When I stepped into Faulkner's office for the first time, I remember slightly stumbling over my words, trying to explain my background and my specific research interest quickly and succinctly, like the one-minute elevator dissertation pitch one hones while on the job market.[5] He welcomed my ideas, signed my consent form, and immediately began talking about some troubles he had teaching his plays to some of the new players. I grabbed my digital recorder and hit play. "Our point guard, Sean [Brennan]," he told me, half whispering in case Brennan were to walk by, "I've even said to him, I've said, 'Sean, I am not going to tell you you have to pass here.' There are some sets where there is a pattern but there are certain sets where I want them to read. It's repetition. Putting them in those spots enough so that they say 'Oh, yeah, I see now.'" And then Faulkner spoke the line that has long stuck with me, a softly spoken, off-handed comment as I put away my recorder: "We're not there yet. I don't know if you ever get there." All these years into being a college basketball coach, Faulkner is still learning how to teach the complex formations, learning how to teach "plays where everything is manipulated" and plays with a "freelance type of thing."

Notes

1. Small portions of this chapter appeared in my article "The Literate Practices of a Division II Men's Basketball Team" in *Grassroots Writing Research Journal* (Rifenburg 2016a), a wonderful journal full of largely undergraduate and graduate-student writing edited by Joyce R. Walker and published by the Illinois State University Writing Program: isuwriting.com.

2. I view student-athletes, in the words of the CCCC Guidelines for the Ethical Conduct of Research in Composition Studies (National Council of Teachers of English 2015), as a population "who may be considered vulnerable and protected" because they have "less institutional power." It may be odd to consider student-athletes in the spotlight of football and basketball as having less institutional power. But student-athletes' lack of autonomy, not to mention their inability to be classified as employees by the National Labor Relations Board or receive direct compensation for their service to their respective schools, worries me as I approach big-time college sports from a researcher's perspective. These students often have someone checking to make sure they are attending class; they have mandatory team meetings, weight-lifting, practices, and media sessions. I spoke with athletic academic advisors who admit to deterring student-athletes from majoring in the hard sciences because afternoon labs would interfere with practice schedules. The athletics department can wield great academic power on university campuses, and suddenly the athletics department is controlling both the *student* and the *athlete* portions of the hyphenated identity marker *student-athlete*. Through their lack of autonomy in basic decisions such as declaring a major and scheduling classes, I view student-athletes as a vulnerable population even though they are not included as such in the listing in the CCCC Guidelines for the Ethical Conduct of Research in Composition Studies or in my own university's guidelines for human-subject research. Therefore, I have tried multiple methods to ensure student-athletes were speaking to me of their own volition and not because they were coerced by a head coach or an athletics department. I have many tales of failing in this attempt, however, which shows the unfortunate position many student-athletes find themselves in: a pawn in the big-business game of College Sports.

3. Throughout this book, I collected all human-subject data with IRB approval and guided by the CCCC Guidelines for the Ethical Conduct of Research in Composition Studies.

4. With permission, all names are people's real names.

5. I had this exact experience while writing my dissertation. I was riding the elevator at CCCC in St. Louis. The elevator stopped at a floor and in walked Mark Emmert, executive director of the NCAA. It was just the two of us, and I had seven floors to introduce myself and my research. I later saw him speak on a panel at CCCC; Martha Townsend organized a great session on college-sports literacy. The then-athletics director of Missouri spoke, as did Emmert.

SECTION II

Teaching Our Student-Athlete Writers

4

HOW CAN WE BETTER TEACH OUR STUDENT-ATHLETE WRITERS (PART 1)?
A Narrative of a Division I Writing Center

*If you think about what we [the athletics department] are doing, there
is nothing more important than having anything and everything we
do reflect back on the number-one priority and that is creating the best
atmosphere for student-athlete academic success.*
> —Joseph R. Castiglione, vice president for
> intercollegiate athletics, director of athletics,
> University of Oklahoma

*The admission, academic standing and academic progress of student-
athletes shall be consistent with the policies and standards adopted by
the institution for the student body in general.*
> —NCAA's Section 2.5, Principle of Sound
> Academic Standards

As a tutor, when I sat down one on one with student-athlete writers on
the third floor of the Gaylord Family Oklahoma Memorial Stadium at the
University of Oklahoma, I worked under an intense athletics-department
gaze, a disinterested NCAA gaze, and an increasingly distrustful public
gaze—all of which led to impotent writing tutoring.[1] Fearful of committing
an NCAA academic violation, the Thompson Writing Center (hereafter,
the *athletics writing center*) staff required student-athletes to submit all their
papers via e-mail in preparation for a face-to-face writing tutoring session.
A tutor uploaded the paper to the plagiarism-detection website Turnitin.
com and stapled the Turnitin.com report to a hard copy of the student-
athlete's paper. Then, in green pen—and always green pen—and with
the student-athlete not present, the tutor marked the paper according to
a coding system printed on laminated lime-green paper: *awk* for awkward
phrasing, # for insert space, *sub/verb* for subject-verb disagreement, and

DOI: 10.7330/9781607326892.c004

so on. The tutor filed the paper and Turnitin.com report away in a bulky, bureaucratic filing cabinet, the drawers separated by sport.

When the student-athlete writer returned according to a scheduled time, they sat with a writing tutor, often not the same one who marked the paper.[2] The tutor pulled the paper and Turnitin.com report from the file cabinet and explained the markings. Like drill-and-practice exercises, which Neal Lerner (1998) explains were features of the laboratory approach to writing instruction in the early twentieth century, these student-athlete tutoring sessions employed a systemized approach to bettering writing, not writers. Following the session, the tutor copied the paper, handed the original to the student-athlete, and returned the copy and Turnitin.com report to the file cabinet in case of an internal or external investigation into potential academic misconduct. Some tutors within the athletics department understood collaborative dialogue between writer and tutor to be effective for literate development, so documenting qualitative data in tidy and transparent Excel spreadsheets was tough for them. Some within the athletics department understood that rote, systematic markings on writing did not lead to better writers, but tutors' aggregating quantitative data on spreadsheets casts an illusion of scientific exactness onto the messy process of tutoring writing. The athletics writing center—a space cut off from campus-wide conversations on student writing—embraced rote, hierarchical tutoring. This tutoring arose because of vague NCAA academic compliance mandates combined with increased scrutiny from external stakeholders.

Though the NCAA loudly bangs the drums of academic integrity and reform, its annually released manuals speak briefly on academics. In August of each year, the NCAA publishes a print and digital copy of a four hundred-plus-page manual. One can order a hard copy or download a free PDF at ncaapublications.com. The NCAA publishes three separate manuals (Division I, II, and III), yet all three only offer one principle directed toward academics. This principle is found in the opening pages under Article 2 of the NCAA Constitution, Principles for Conduct of Intercollege Athletics and, wedged between a The Principle of Sportsmanship and The Principle of Nondiscrimination, is Section 2.5, The Principle of Sound Academic Standards. It reads, "Intercollegiate athletics programs shall be maintained as a vital component of the educational program, and student-athletes shall be an integral part of the student body. The admission, academic standing and academic progress of student-athletes shall be consistent with the policies and standards adopted by the institution for the student body in general" (National Collegiate Athletic Association 2017a).

The NCAA provides a follow-up to Section 2.5 in Section 16.3, titled "Academic Counseling/Support Services." However, this section seems to repeat previously covered content in Section 2.5 and still leaves exactly what this implementation should look like up to individual schools.

> **16.3.1.1 Academic Counseling/Support Services.** Member institutions shall make general academic counseling and tutoring services available to all student-athletes. Such counseling and tutoring services may be provided by the department of athletics or the institution's nonathletics student support services. In addition, an institution, conference or the NCAA may finance other academic support, career counseling or personal development services that support the success of student-athletes.

The NCAA places the responsibility of academic-policy creation, implementation, and enforcement on individual institutions through the vague construction of the two-sentence Section 2.5. The University of Oklahoma (OU) struggled with this lack of direction from college sports' multimillion-dollar governing body.

In chapter 2, I describe what plays are and what do they do. In chapter 3, through a narrative of a season with the men's basketball team at the University of North Georgia, I argue players leverage three cognitive processes (haptic communication, scaffolded situations, and spatial orientation) to learn the scripted plays of their sport. These next two chapters connect with the first two by describing how we can better teach our student-athletes in writing-intensive spaces like FYC or a writing center based on implementing what we know about how they learn. The initial challenge to such implementation, however, is the material circumstances. Student-athletes, more so than most students we encounter, are caught in a sticky web of matrices and policies spun by the NCAA, the athletics department's conference, and the athletics department itself. This web traps the student-athlete, often stripping them of curricular and extracurricular agency. One slight tug on any of the silken threads by, say, the athletics department jostles the student-athlete in that desired direction. I don't want to push this arachnid metaphor too far but contribute this image to argue that the initial step toward teaching or tutoring student-athletes is to develop an acute awareness of these matrices and policies— and not adopt an insouciant or flippant attitude as can so often be the case when faculty find student-athletes enrolled in their classes. Working with student-athlete writers does not begin by wiping the web away with a broom, thus allowing the student-athlete to fly free. Working with student-athlete writers begins by seeing the web and learning—sometimes with the student-athlete—how to move with and not necessarily against the complex patterns of the web holding NCAA student-athletes.

In this chapter, I turn to this web; I turn to the material circumstances in which student-athlete writing instruction—in a writing center, as is the specific case for this chapter, or in any writing-intensive space—occurs. We know three cognitive practices student-athletes deploy to engage with writing in their sports, but implementing these practices in a writing-intensive curricular space demands we first understand and then work with the many academic and student-life matrices and policies governing how student-athletes move through US higher education under the aegis of the NCAA. Working with student-athlete writers is a lot more than just motivating the potentially unmotivated and navigating around missed classes due to practices and games. Working with student-athlete writers, no matter how refined our theories and practices, begins and ends by working with our and their material circumstances.

I offer my experience working in two different writing centers at OU, a prominent research university with an even more prominent athletics department. For four years, I worked as a program-development coordinator in the athletics writing center; for two years, I worked as a lead tutor in the campus-wide writing center. In my position with the athletics department, I hired and trained English and writing tutors for OU student-athletes and designed and ran monthly training sessions in accordance with our College Reading and Learning Association Level 2 certification. However, even though the athletics department knew its student-athletes, NCAA academic-compliance mandates handcuffed the athletics writing center to outdated methods of working with writers. Just knowing our students and acknowledging their prior knowledge isn't enough. Implementing pedagogies inspired by knowing our students is fraught with programmatic and pedagogical challenges, particularly when this implementation occurs under the NCAA's watch.

Through in-person and e-mail interviews with three participants operating at various levels within the athletics writing center—including the director of athletics quoted in the epigraph—and textual analysis of documents outlining policy and procedures within the athletics writing center, I describe the constrictive material circumstances in which the athletics writing center found itself and how my participants perceived and enacted student-athlete tutoring services based on these circumstances. The athletics center initially handcuffed itself to outdated methods of working with student-athlete writers because of a zealous (yet understandable) commitment to preventing NCAA academic misconduct. Instead of writing yet another dour narrative on college sports and academics, I describe how this athletics writing center formed intra-institutional alliances with campus WPAs within the campus-wide writing center to improve writing tutoring for student-athletes. Ultimately, I erect a foundation onto which we can build and implement pedagogies driven by how student-athletes learn, which is explicated in chapter 3.

I turn attention to the writing center and the material challenges therein because I see the work of writing centers as representative of the larger work animating the daily professional lives of those of us devoted to college-level writing instruction: advocating for writing and writers within and against the larger tides of academic change washing over our campuses; sitting with a writer and wrangling recalcitrant prose; implementing best practices galvanized by our conference presentations, journal articles, listserv discussions, and serendipitous hallway conversations with colleagues. When we talk about the work of the writing center, we are talking about all our collective work, an earnest commitment to writers and writing erected on a foundation of material circumstances directly affecting writers and writing.

(THE) MATERIAL MATTERS: THE WHO, WHAT, WHEN, AND WHERE OF STUDENT-ATHLETE WRITING TUTORING

The University of Oklahoma is a Division I public research university, classified by the Carnegie Foundation as a Research University/High Activity. With roughly thirty thousand total students and an endowment of over $1.4 billion, this doctoral-granting university prides itself on academics. When I began data collection, according to the OU Office of Institutional Research and Reporting, the 4,052 first-time first-year students entered with an average ACT score of 25.5 and an average SAT score of 1186, and 32.7 percent had graduated in the top 10 percent of their high-school class.

OU also prides itself on its athletic success. With nineteen varsity sports, OU has notched thirty-two national-championship trophies in team sports. Individual success supports this team success. Five football players have won the Heisman trophy, given annually to the best college football player in the nation, and are immortalized with towering bronze statues outside the stadium. In 2009, the Los Angeles Clippers selected Blake Griffin with the first pick in the NBA draft, and the following year—when I was busy working with OU student-athlete writers—the St. Louis Rams selected Sam Bradford with the first pick in the NFL draft. More important, OU is one of the few athletics programs in the nation with a self-sustaining budget of around $120 million annually.[3] According to the 2014–2015 Oklahoma Athletics Annual Report, the department tallied a revenue of $120,500,000 against expenses of

$120,430,000 (University of Oklahoma Department of Intercollegiate Athletics 2015). The football team alone is responsible for generating 29 percent of this revenue, costing 21 percent of the total budget. At a time when athletics departments offer few examples of fiscal responsibility and rely on student fees to field teams, OU athletics is self-sustaining and contributes financially to the general academic mission of the school. Through increased revenue under athletic director Joseph Castiglione, whom I interviewed for this chapter, OU enlarged its student-athlete academic and student-life services. These services are found under the umbrella of Athletic Student Life (ASL).

ASL contains a wealth of student life and academic services dedicated to its roughly six hundred student-athletes: career services, the psychological-resource center, the math center, the Kerr Foundation Foreign Language Center, the dining hall, housing, and the Thompson Writing Center (what I am calling in this chapter, for clarity, the *athletics writing center*). The athletics writing center is a relatively small space on the second floor of the football stadium with five round tables with four chairs each and a table lining the wall supporting four desktop computers. Four cubicles, used by graduate assistants, including myself for four years, line the back wall. Two enclosed offices occupied by full-time staff face the only door in and out of the space. During my time in the center, I worked with four other writing tutors. Three of the four were students (two graduate students and one undergraduate), and one was a community member.

Student-athletes were welcome to visit the campus-wide writing center. That said, most preferred the proximity of the athletics writing center. Unlike the OU Writing Center (hereafter, *campus-wide writing center*), the athletics writing center does not position itself as a space where student-athletes can freely write and study. The center does not hold events throughout the semester, provide water, tea, or coffee to writers, or advertise its services in the campus newspaper and various social media platforms. It doesn't need to seek out writers; writers (i.e., student-athlete writers) are required to use the services. Once a writing tutoring session is complete, tutors ask student-athletes to leave.

The campus-wide writing center sits roughly 150 yards away from the athletics writing center. Under the direction of Michele Eodice, the campus-wide writing center has a strong presence on campus through multiple satellite locations, regularly updated social media content, and frequent campus activities including Waffles for Writers and Shut Up & Write. The campus-wide writing center is open to all writers, from faculty members to community members, and offers face-to-face, synchronous, and asynchronous writing support.

Moving between the athletics writing center and the campus-wide writing center during my time as a doctoral candidate, I engaged in ongoing dialogue with tutors and administrators. With IRB approval and guided by the 2015 CCCC Guidelines for the Ethical Conduct of Research in Composition Studies, all my participants had the option of e-mail or in-person semistructured interviews. In this chapter, I listen to the voices of three participants, three stakeholders in the OU athletics writing center:

- Joseph Castiglione, vice president for intercollegiate athletics, director of athletics. A former student-athlete at Maryland, Castiglione arrived as the vice president for intercollegiate athletics, director of athletics, at OU in 1998, oversaw the second renovation of the academic center in 2002, and now governs an annual self-sustaining athletics budget of nearly $100 million. Under his guidance, OU developed a career center, psychological-resource office, and writing center solely for student-athlete use.

- Brooke Clevenger, tutoring coordinator. Clevenger was finishing her first year as a full-time staff member prior to my data collection. Clevenger worked within athletic academic services while completing her MEd degree in adult and higher education with an emphasis in intercollegiate athletics administration. Following completion of her degree, Clevenger landed a full-time staff position as tutorial coordinator responsible for coordinating the student-athletes' and tutors' schedules for all subjects except math and foreign language.

- Andrew Russo, writing tutor in the athletics writing center. At the time of data collection, Russo was finishing his dissertation in philosophy and was on the job market. This was his first year as a writing tutor. Though he did not have experience as a writing tutor, his strong commitment to teaching and undergraduate learning positioned him well as one of four student-athlete writing tutors.

- Lena Erickson, writing consultant in the campus-wide writing center. Erickson was a second-year student majoring in math. During data collection, Erickson was completing her first year in the writing center.

- Mike Mohon, writing consultant in the campus-wide writing center. Mike had long worked in the writing center, first as an undergrad and, during the time of data collection, as a second-year MA candidate in the composition/rhetoric/literacy program housed in the English Department.

INSIDE THE OU ATHLETICS WRITING CENTER: A MISSION OF PREVENTING ACADEMIC MISCONDUCT

Avoiding academic misconduct is the central goal of the athletics writing center. This goal is achieved through policies and practices dictating how to work with student-athlete writers and policies and practices describing the atmosphere in which this work will occur. As Castiglione told me during our two-hour in-person interview, "There are several ways [one] can violate NCAA rules, but the most hurtful to a program is blatant academic misconduct."[4] Such a direct statement from the athletics director trickled down to Clevenger and Russo. Clevenger, in an e-mail response, wrote that "both the NCAA and compliance have to protect the institution and its athletics department first," and Russo used a form of the verb *to prevent* six times and the phrase "academic misconduct" four times in his e-mail response.[5] Blatant academic misconduct leads to an NCAA investigation and often a forfeiture of wins, postseason play, and scholarships. Blatant academic misconduct might also spell the end of a student-athlete's career, which can in turn devastate a program and cut into the dollars a program may earn. When a high-profile player in a high-profile sport comes into the athletics writing center, the preventive posturing is ratcheted up a notch in hopes of ensuring the player's continual eligibility and the lucrative longevity of the program and the large athletics department. This preventive posturing is borne at two levels: locally with the compliance department and nationally with the NCAA.

The compliance department, which Clevenger mentioned, enforces these preventive responsibilities through monitoring social media sites, coordinating potential future student-athlete campus visits, checking student-athlete daily classroom attendance, and monitoring an anonymous phone line and e-mail address to report potential violations. Located one floor above the athletics writing center, this nine-person compliance department is made up largely of people with law backgrounds and reports directly to the NCAA; therefore, the compliance department does not appear on the organizational chart for the athletics department as found via the Office of Institutional Research and Reporting. Despite compliance's organizational distance from the athletics writing center, the department is able to keep a close watch on the activities within the space through holding three staff-wide meetings a year (which I detail shortly) and sending periodic e-mails reminding all staff members of academic-compliance mandates.

The tone compliance sets for the athletics writing center finds its root in the second half of compliance's vision statement found as a PDF online: "The [OU] Athletics Compliance Department will strive to decrease secondary violations through education and monitoring while remaining vigilant in our efforts to report instances where compliance was not achieved and implementing appropriate corrective measures when necessary" (University of Oklahoma 2018).

"Vigilant" and "appropriate corrective measures" smart of policing, not educating. Because of this policing, the athletics writing center finds itself in an odd position of responding to a dictum given by compliance, a dictum given out of fear of academic misconduct and not an interest in pedagogical advancement. As Clevenger wrote, "[Tutors] must be cautious in offering 'too much' help," and "abiding by lengthy manuals of procedures and rules leaves no room for error for either the student-athletes or the faculty and staff members." Required compliance meetings provide an overview of the lengthy manuals and procedures Clevenger describes. I attended these meetings numerous times. The director of compliance walked hundreds of people in the audience through numerous PowerPoint slides. Compliance required us to sign a paper acknowledging our attendance and awareness of NCAA academic-compliance mandates and local compliance mandates.

One can see how Russo focuses on preventive responsibilities in his response because of the gravity of these meetings: "Consequences for academic behavior," "stop academic misconduct," "preventive responsibilities," "preventive character," and so on. Russo even writes that the "primary responsibility as writing tutors here is preventive." It is worth noting, however, that at times Russo leverages "preventive" to consider accidental plagiarism and grammatical and mechanical missteps in a student-athlete's writing. For Clevenger and Castiglione, preventive measures defend against academic fraud. While Russo too is on the watch for academic fraud, he also looks to "fix misconceptions about plagiarism and remedy bad habits to produce better, more responsible college writers" and to "stop bad writing habits before the SA's get too far along in their college careers." Such phrases again draw attention to the drill-and-practice approach to writing instruction espoused by the athletics writing center.

During my interview with Castiglione, I expressed concern with what I perceive to be compliance dictating pedagogy. He replied,

> I think you raise a fair point. Compliance isn't making decisions about what we do in academic services as long as it's in compliance with the NCAA rules. And they are there to ensure there is ongoing monitoring and checks and balances in place so that someone doesn't go astray. There are several ways we can violate NCAA rules but the most hurtful to a program is blatant academic fraud. And even as intentional as we are about integrity and trying to do the right thing, people with intent on doing something wrong can find a way to beat the system eventually. . . . Having said that doesn't mean that [compliance] gets involved with determining academic initiatives. If there are some that send out a threat from a compliance standpoint, we will run it by them.

I pushed a bit more in a follow-up observation: "To speak candidly, sometimes [in the athletics writing center] we are frustrated because we feel compliance is more concerned about us not breaking rules than they are about us helping the student-athletes." Castiglione replied, "Fair question, and being very blunt, it is something we need to watch. It doesn't mean we don't want the strict compliance with the rule, and we don't want to be proactive in protecting ourselves. But we are here to promote education."

In his response, Castiglione operates proactively by wanting to ensure "integrity" despite people "intent on doing something wrong." I see compliance as disruptive to pedagogical advancement; Castiglione sees compliance as a necessary protective element against a "threat." Though I agree with Castiglione, it is unfortunate a writing center must actively position itself with a group using a policing gaze.

At the national level, the preventive posturing comes from the NCAA, specifically Section 2.5: The Principle of Sound Academic Standards. The principle is vague because the NCAA is not fully sure how academics should operate inside athletics departments, particularly at the high-stakes and high-dollar level of Division I athletics. As a result, they leave it up to individual athletics departments. Some may argue the principle is not vague but rather malleable enough to fit the needs of individual member institutions. Or that the NCAA is respecting the sovereignty of each member institution because NCAA membership is voluntary. However, the NCAA articulates seven core values. The first reads that the NCAA is committed to "the collegiate model of athletics in which students participate as an avocation, balancing their academic, social, and athletics experiences" (National Collegiate Athletic Association 2017a). Out of the seven core values, three speak directly to academics. Yet only one statement in the NCAA manuals manifests this purpose and these values. The manuals do not provide a section detailing how to work *academically* with a student-athlete. To be fair, the NCAA strongly promotes the autonomy of member institutions. One of their seven core values reads, "Respect for institutional autonomy and philosophical differences" (National Collegiate Athletic Association 2017a). It is also worth remembering that membership in the NCAA is voluntary. Therefore, the creation and ultimate enforcement of academic policy is up to individual institutions (i.e., the institution's compliance department). As a result, the OU compliance department decides how one can academically work with the roughly six hundred student-athletes. The compliance department casts a heavy gaze over academics because of fear of academic fraud. This gaze encourages rote, hierarchical tutoring and form after form after form.

Mike Mohon, a second year MA student working in the campus-wide writing center, offers a different understanding of tutoring, tutoring free from the constraints imposed by the athletics department and NCAA mandates: "When working with our guests, we need to keep both points simultaneously in mind. We don't just check grammar or just ask questions; we do both, with our eyes on both goals. In the OU Writing Center, we are more trained and encouraged in helping students with thinking about their writing, but we don't neglect mechanical issues. We learn quite a bit of theory to that end, from the prerequisite course we take to be eligible for the job, to practicums, conferences and conversations."

For Mohon, "Creativity and hard work" is an outcome of "high standards with flexible guidelines." His response signals the collaborative atmosphere of the campus-wide writing center. Clevenger and Russo never use the plural pronoun we, as Mohon does when describing the athletics writing center. Though Russo does mention "our," Mohon relies heavily on the collective plural pronoun. Though I am looking at a small sample size, it is worth noting that the writing center with the "lack of structure" causes a tutor to speak more of the collective collaborative *we* and not the lone *I* heavily used by Russo when describing his "preventive" responsibilities.

Finally, Mohon's pedagogical focuses clashes with Clevenger's. Mohon writes, "We need to help people," but Clevenger leans more toward the belief that tutors are "hired to supplement," and Russo writes of the preventative nature of student-athlete writing tutoring. Through Mohon's response, we are looking at a creative, free-flowing writing center, which aids in collaboration, a space to "grow as an intellectual and as a professional."

Erickson articulates a similar read of the atmosphere of the campus-wide writing center, even though she had worked in the space for less than a semester when she wrote this response for me. Erickson's response is the shortest I received yet is full of reflection. I provide it in full.

> When I first came to the Writing Center as a student, I immediately felt an attraction to the space, which buzzed with enthusiasm for intellectual challenge and growth. Consultants counter-argued my points and gave honest feedback. They connected me to resources. They made me think a little differently each time I came. It wasn't until I took the Working with Writers course and became a writing consultant that I realized how much improvisation it takes to do all this.[6] A lot of thought goes into maintaining this space that encourages freedom in scholarly discourse. People come to the Writing Center to learn rules of writing in various communities, but also to break the rules, become more original, and develop their

own style and content to offer the world. This whole process roots itself in candid, friendly discussion and is nurtured by the director's [Michele Eodice's] insistence on liberty to make mistakes in order to learn.

Like Mohon, Erickson keys in on the unique atmosphere of the space. Words such as "buzzed," "freedom," and "original" drive her response. And like Mohon's, Erickson's response seems strongly informed by the collaborative and free-flowing atmosphere created by Eodice and her staff. Erickson writes of Eodice's "insistence on liberty to make mistakes in order to learn." Finally, Erickson writes the campus-wide writing center helps writers learn the rules governing the discourses in their disciplines and then ways to stretch and play with those rules. This idea of teaching learners how to "stretch and play with those rules" connects back to chapter 3 and how the head basketball coach at the University of North Georgia, Chris Faulkner, teaches scripted plays. Faulkner designs a system in which he wants his players to operate but also stresses how to improvise within this system. As one player on the team, Travis Core, told me, "I know [Faulkner] yells at us sometimes for running the play robotically." Faulkner does not want robotic players, and the campus-wide writing center at OU does not want to develop robotic writers. The fluid rhetorical situations surrounding college writing and college basketball demand malleable constructs in which rhetors make rhetorically sound decisions. But material circumstances at the athletics writing center do not create an atmosphere that facilitates or encourages malleable constructs for its student-athletes. In the next chapter, I dig deeper into this idea of improvising within a given rhetorical construct by turning to elements of jazz improvisation that scholars in a variety of disciplines extend to other learning contexts. But here I point to a glaring difference between the campus-wide writing center and the athletics writing center: how each space creates an atmosphere that facilitates or quells malleable writing constructs.

Creating an atmosphere allowing for control supports the importance of preventing academic misconduct. Clevenger's language in her written response is striking, particularly her opening sentence in which she writes, "First and foremost, a tutor needs to keep in mind [their] primary duties. Tutors have been hired to supplement what the student has already learned in class." Glossing over this language, one gets the sense that tutoring support for Division I athletics is a business. Clevenger's language feels like a contract detailing employee duties. Such documents can be helpful. But this language imbues the athletics writing center, dictates its everyday practices, and prescribes the atmosphere of the athletics writing center. The athletics writing center refrigerates ideas; it does not incubate ideas.

Such language is influenced by (or influences) the atmosphere in which student-athlete writing tutoring occurs. Like Clevenger, Russo describes this atmosphere. In his second paragraph, Russo moves toward describing a stop-gap approach to student-athlete writing tutoring in which the responsibility to quell "bad writing" habits of student-athletes resides with the student-athlete writing tutors: "In my mind, our primary responsibility as writing tutors here is preventive. Stop academic misconduct before it makes it's way to campus where the consequences are more dire. Stop bad writing habits before the SA's get too far along in their college careers. The regulations and rules dictate what are and are not appropriate ways to work with a student-athlete and do not leave much room to cultivate good writing techniques. Rather our job, as I see it, is to block the 'bad' rather than foster the 'good.'"

Like Clevenger, Russo positions the primary job of a student-athlete writing tutor at the forefront of his response. Russo does acknowledge that "the regulations and rules . . . do not leave much room to cultivate good writing techniques"; however, I am taken by how acutely this preventative approach plays into how he works with writers. Here is a bind: as a graduate teaching assistant in the philosophy department and as one actively writing his teaching philosophy and on the job market during my data collection, Russo appears to want to "cultivate good writing techniques." Despite Russo's well-intentioned desire of cultivation, the incessant monitoring, the vague NCAA compliance mandates, and the atmosphere of preventing misconduct over facilitating learning force him into a defensive posture.

The The Prentice Gautt Tutoring & Learning Specialist Program manual additionally influences Clevenger's and Russo's responses.[7] Following a letter from Gerald Gurney, the Senior Associate Athletics Director for Academics & Student Life, an Equal Opportunity Statement, and a brief bio on the former student-athlete and professional athlete after whom the space is named, the manual leads with "Rules, Policies & Procedures." This section touches on sports wagering and sexual harassment, as well as the dress code and the use of the Internet and the copy machine. The next section dictates how tutors should interact with student-athletes, an interaction that stems from compliance's interpretation of the vague NCAA Constitution's Section 2.5. Stipulating that "tutoring sessions are designed to provide assistance for student-athletes in order to enhance the chances of academic success," the program lists five tutor responsibilities:

- Develop a subject-centered educational plan for the best academic potential in your student-athlete.
- Create realistic and content driven subject level learning goals with the student-athlete.
- Encourage the student-athlete to keep an open line of communication with the professor.
- Focus only on your content area.
- Report if the student-athlete hasn't completed necessary reading and preparation to make the session meaningful. (22)

The first three responsibilities are quite helpful. Though the fourth strikes me as a bit odd, I can understand the reasoning. Based on my experience, the final responsibility is the most critical responsibility for a tutor in the athletics writing center, and it reflects the desired atmosphere of the space: one of control, of policing. I appreciate the intentions behind these responsibilities. Unfortunately, the final responsibility shows the athletics writing center operating from a fear of academic misconduct. One gets the sense of entering a doctor's office when walking into the student-athlete writing center. Silence abounds. Month-old copies of *Sports Illustrated* and *Entertainment Weekly* sit in the corner. Student-athletes in sweatpants and Nike Dri-FIT shirts sit huddled over their phones, bottles of half-finished Gatorade on the table. During a thirty-minute session, student-athletes sign multiple forms, adding their ID numbers and sports.

This atmosphere counters what Elizabeth Boquet (2002) describes in *Noise from the Writing Center*: "We [writing center consultants and administrators] must imagine a liminal zone where chaos and order coexist. And we would certainly do a service to ourselves . . . if we spent as much time championing this chaos . . . as we do championing the order" (84). In Boquet's space, consultants and administrators consider conventions and, if needed, adapt conventions to meet the rhetorical demands of twenty-first-century composing. She muses that her strong commitment to balancing chaos and order may "perhaps be why I resist to such a degree the idea of scripted performance in the writing center" (83). Instead, Boquet thinks of writing center work as "controlled chaos . . . a frame that enables me, in my work with writers, to acknowledge the importance of preparation while at the same time immersing myself in the pleasure of the here and now" (83–84). Boquet's words work on two levels for my purposes. First, her understanding of writing center work through the metaphors of noise and music links up with my next chapter, in which I also look to music, specifically jazz improvisation, as a conceptual framework for working with student-athlete writers. Boquet hints at improvisation with her nod to the "here and now" over "scripted performance." Again, I pick up this thread more directly in the next chapter but point to it briefly here. On the other more immediate level, Boquet's admission of championing order *and* chaos strikes a disharmonic melody in comparison to that played by the athletics department. Imagine providing Boquet's chaos/order amalgamation to a lawyer running the compliance department at a high-profile Division I university. The compliance department would run from such a suggestion, not understanding that theory, practice, and effectiveness ground Boquet's statement. The athletics writing center lies stagnant in an unproductive struggle under the weight of preventive posturing and does not embrace chaos/order.

The preventive posturing is, ostensibly, in the best interest of the student-athlete. But the student-athlete, the living, breathing, learning writer, is the one forgotten. To riff on Stephen North's (1984) well-known argument, the policies strive toward better writing and not better writers. The student-athletes are forgotten. I think of the star offensive player from southern California, tattoos coiling around his corded biceps, his hair bleached blond and sticking straight up, his skateboard flipped upside down on a table. Now playing in the NFL, he is a strong writer who authored strong prose and received the occasional *awk* marking above his words but who never received—at least in the athletics writing center—writing tutoring in line with current best practices. Forgotten, too, is the large defensive player from Texas. I remember his powerful frame hunched over a sheet of paper as he scratched out word after word after word. In a basso tone, he told me his plan after graduating: cutting hair in Dallas or playing in the league. Unsure of how to respond to such a direct statement balancing two extremes, I turned back to his writing, explaining the green markings as he fiddled with his goatee.

These are the material circumstances in which student-athlete writing tutoring exists. Many of the agents contributing to the scene of student-athlete writing tutoring cannot be replaced. The answer to bettering this scene is not ignoring the agents that are the NCAA, the compliance department, the athletics department. To improve this scene, we don't need to change the agents. We need to add another agent, an agent committed to writing center best practices. I introduce this agent in the next section.

INSIDE THE OU ATHLETICS WRITING CENTER: THE MATERIAL CHALLENGES OF IMPROVING WRITING INSTRUCTION

In hopes of improving this atmosphere of forgetting the writer for the sake of an aura of academic integrity, the athletics writing center connected with Michele Eodice, the director of the campus-wide writing center, and upper-level athletic and academic administrators. This connection resulted in two changes within the athletics writing center during the summer of 2010 and illustrates the importance of forming intra-institutional relationships in order to establish best practices in learning while still adhering to important NCAA mandates. These changes were seismic shifts in tutoring philosophies and practices. As at other writing centers undergoing similar seismic shifts, even though the changes were needed, administrators and tutors struggled to adapt. Michele Eodice, Associate Provost for Academic Engagement and Director of the campus-wide writing center, Moira Ozias, the Associate Director, and Evan Chambers, a Program Assistant, surveyed fifty-seven peer institutions to learn about writing-related services offered to student-athletes, specifically online writing assistance. Thirty institutions responded, and Eodice spearheaded a report detailing the findings. These findings and recommendations were disseminated to the faculty athletics representative and athletics academic services. Persuaded by the report and the pedagogical effectiveness of online writing tutoring, the faculty athletics representative drafted a memo calling for the OU athletics writing center to adopt asynchronous writing tutoring via the track changes and commenting functions of Microsoft Word. This first change—adopting asynchronous writing tutoring—is especially helpful for student-athletes traveling or injured and physically unable to visit the athletics writing center.

Second, the athletics writing center overturned the nearly decade-long adherence to the green pens and laminated lime-green coded sheet and moved toward a collaborative writing session between writer and tutor. After the Eodice report convinced athletic administrators that the athletics writing center would not be offering extra academic benefits to student-athletes if its model of writing tutoring mirrored that of the campus-wide writing center and peer institutions, student-athlete tutors were able to cover global concerns in student-athlete writing. Student-athletes no longer came in after a tutor read and marked their papers. Instead, student-athlete and tutor collaboratively set the agenda and moved past solely remarking on usage, punctuation, and "awk" sentence construction. However, because of the harsh penalties often accompanying academic misconduct, Turnitin.com is still a mainstay in the athletics writing center, despite a CCCC resolution voicing opposition against plagiarism-detection services like Turnitin.com (DelliCarpini 2013, 377–78) and the campus-wide writing center's not adopting its use.

In sum, the material circumstances in which student-athlete writing tutoring occurs negatively constricts writing tutoring to bettering prose at the risk of forgetting the writer. These material circumstances arise for two causal reasons: the NCAA authors vague academic compliance mandates with harsh financial and athletic penalties waiting for infractions; therefore, individual schools are forced to interpret individually these mandates and, understandably and unfortunately, err on the side of caution, thus curbing best practices in working with writers. My description of the two writing centers at OU is a case study in how to ameliorate—to some degree—the constrictive environment of student-athlete writing instruction. Alliances between people committed to student writing illustrate the need for writing center scholars to use their collective capacity to advocate for strong writing-related academic services for all students. Such collaborative work is illustrative of what Jane Nelson and Margaret Garner (2011) refer to as "horizontal structures of learning" in their description of the University of Wyoming Writing Center. Through a horizontal structure of learning, individual departments or campus academic services do not delegate the role of facilitating student engagement and deep learning. Instead, through establishing "meaningful and productive relationships with people across campus" (10), all share a commitment to implementing and facilitating best practices for student learning. Under a horizontal structure of learning, then, the responsibility of student-athlete writing support does not fall solely on the shoulders of the athletics department; all campus stakeholders share the responsibility.

EXPANDING OUR GAZE AND BETTERING OUR PRACTICES

So how can we better teach student-athlete writers? By returning to the ambiguous Section 2.5. This Section is the initial step toward better student-athlete writing instruction and ensuring the writing practices espoused by the athletics writing center are the *policies and standards adopted by the institution for the student body in general.* Once that is in place, we can move more directly toward helping student-athletes transfer their learning from the court to the classroom.

According to the NCAA's own language, if the whole OU campus adopts the campus-wide writing center' view of writing instruction, the athletics writing center must. If our student-athletes are to receive quality writing support, we must build bridges to athletics departments and show that the principles we implement in our writing center are the *policies and standards adopted by the institution for the student body in general.* For our work to be the standard, we must make intra-institutional connections. An athletics writing center removed from campus conversations on student writing and tutoring is not operating in the best interests of campus stakeholders. Yet an isolated athletics writing center is common within high-profile athletics departments and is often cast positively by athletics-department stakeholders. In her article on writing tutoring for football student-athletes at Texas, Alanna Bitzel (2012) writes of the location of these tutoring sessions: "[The center] is removed from and not accessible to the rest of campus, emphasizing that at least one part of the student-athletes' lives is not available for perusal" (para. 4). I appreciate the desire to keep high-profile student-athletes out of the constant spotlight and allow them to concentrate on their studies. That said, I have concerns with what I perceive to be insular athletics writing centers. A writing center cut off from the rest of campus does not allow the writing center to "serve as the focal point for establishing a culture of writing on campus and in the larger community" (37), a phrase Emily Isaacs and Melinda Knight (2014) use to describe the new models of writing centers they extol.

I doubt high-profile athletics writing centers seek to be these focal points described by Isaacs and Knight. Yet, this narrow understanding of what a writing center can and should do is what Jackie Grutsch McKinney (2013) critiques in *Peripheral Visions for Writing Center Work*. She pushes against what she calls the "grand narrative" of writing centers: "writing centers as *comfortable, iconoclastic places where all students go to get one-to-one tutoring on their writing*" (5). Grutsch McKinney's frustration with this grand narrative is akin to the critique leveled by Anne Ellen Geller, Michele Eodice, Frankie Condon, Meg Carroll, and Elizabeth H. Boquet in *The Everyday Writing Center*. The coauthors worry about the "neatly-packaged representations of our rich, multi-layered, everyday writing center lives" (Geller et al. 2007, 8). Through altering this grand narrative and suggesting how it privileges certain activities while ignoring others, Grutsch McKinney expands the vision of writing centers and provides a foundation through which writing centers and writing center scholarship can adapt to the ever-evolving landscape of US higher education. Not only do campus writing centers need to push against this grand narrative, but so too do athletics writing centers.

In her penultimate chapter, Grutsch McKinney turns to the portion of the grand narrative stating writing centers should only focus on tutoring. Conversely, she argues writing center scholars and scholarship have "hardly started recognizing the scope of what is already done in the writing center" (80). In other words, we already do that something else; we already, say, advocate for all students and establish vital intra-institutional connections, which allow for quality instruction in writing-intensive courses. Unfortunately, since the grand narrative we so often spin doesn't include this something else, we fail to talk and write about it, fail to make it a part of who we are. As Grutsch McKinney writes, the narrative "does not fully represent the possibility, promise, or actuality of our work" (80). We can represent this possibility, promise, and actuality of our work by heeding Grutsch McKinney's call and recognizing the scope of what we are already doing.

Writing center studies can counter this grand narrative by advocating for athletics writing centers and the half-million student-athlete writers on our campuses. When we begin doing more by advocating for our student-athlete writers, we have the opportunity to ensure that campus-wide conversations about what writing is, how it is taught, and how it is assessed are conversations also heard by the athletics department, and that implications are felt in that department. When we advocate for more by remembering our student-athlete writers, we bring these campus-wide conversations about writing to bear on our work with athletics departments and individual student-athlete writers because, returning to the NCAA's own language in Section 2.5, the athletics department's work with writers "shall be consistent" with campus-wide work with writers. Writing center stakeholders are the ones to demand this consistency. And when we strive for this consistency, student-athlete writing tutoring becomes more than simply helping a high-level recruits remain academically eligible.

On a practical level, I close with four implications for writing center administrators, staff, and tutors:

- Writing center administrators, staff, and tutors should advocate for a proper academic atmosphere for student-athletes by gaining familiarity with national athletic academic-reform organizations such as the Knight Commission on Intercollegiate Athletics, the Drake Group, and the Coalition on Intercollegiate Athletics. These groups do not always agree on the best method for academically advocating for student-athletes; however, the steady stream of white papers, policy statements, and research reports complete with best practices authored by these organizations provide qualitative and quantitative data helpful in constructing a case for improving academic conditions for student-athletes.

- Writing center administrators and staff working in separate writing centers for student-athletes can ensure their policies in place mirror those policies in place in the campus-wide writing center. Starting and sustaining collaborative dialogue with the person overseeing the campus-wide writing center can provide a glimpse into the pedagogical practices undergirding that space.

- Again, for campuses with a separate athletics writing center, tutors can work in the campus-wide writing center *and* the athletics writing center. During my time at OU, I and other tutors split our time between these two writing centers. Cross-pollination ensures the policies in place in one space mirror those in the other. In addition, it provides tutors a chance to engage with student-athletes, a population that often feels isolated from the student body and campus (Bell 2009, 34; Tracey and Corlett 1995, 90, 95).

- For campuses with only one writing center visited by all students, writing center administrators, staff, and tutors should learn how NCAA academic policy is enacted and enforced on their campus. They can gain this knowledge by connecting with the faculty athletics representative or the athletics department administration. Regardless of whether the campus writing center is connected with the athletics department, NCAA academic policy must be followed. Understanding these policies and how to work closely with student-athlete writers under these policies is in the best interests of all.

These implications are in the best interests of the four hundred thousand-plus student-athletes in our writing centers, in our classrooms. But we can only work with student-athlete writers better when we improve their material circumstances.

Notes

1. A version of this chapter appeared as "Supporting the Student-Athlete Writer: A Case Study of a Division I Athletics Writing Centers and NCAA Academic Mandates," published in *The Writing Center Journal* (Rifenburg 2016c).
2. In accordance with the move toward gender-neutral language in publications (for example, see Michele Eodice, Steve Price, and Kerri Jordan's editors' introduction to *The Writing Center Journal* [Eodice, Price, and Jordan 2014]), I adopt *they* as a gender-neutral term.
3. According to a 2013 *USA Today* article, Oklahoma is 1 of 8 out of 228 total public Division I universities with a self-sustaining athletics department (Berkowitz, Upton, and Brady 2013).
4. I have slightly edited excerpts from the in-person interview with Castiglione. I omitted false starts and added punctuation and capitalization. For the complete transcript of my interview with Castiglione, see my website mrifenburg.wordpress.com. Under Research, click on A Division 1 Athletics Director Speaks.
5. I only edited excerpts from e-mail interview responses with Brooke and Andrew to clarify pronouns when the antecedent is unclear.
6. English 3193: Working with Writers is a May summer-session course cotaught by Michele Eodice and Moira Ozias, the associate director of the OU Writing Center. During the course, Eodice and Ozias introduce students to theories and practices of writing, as well as how to respond effectively to a writer's prose. Students observe and reflect on writing-consulting sessions in the writing center and practice giving writing feedback to classmates. Though consultants in the OU writing center are not required to take the Working with Writers course, a large number of graduates of the class go on to work in the writing center.
7. For full disclosure, I authored portions of this manual.

5

HOW CAN WE BETTER TEACH OUR STUDENT-ATHLETE WRITERS (PART 2)?
Writing Practices as Jazzy, Creative, Collaborative

Both the improvising jazz musician and the athlete must train intensely to build up sets of conditioned reflexes that enable them to respond without thinking to events that are unfolding around them in fractions of seconds. . . . Like the athlete, [the jazz musician] must deal with them now.
> —James Lincoln Collier

As far as on the court, we give them a framework as to how to play and let them play within that. We are not where you have to stand here, you gotta do this, you gotta do that.
> —University of North Georgia head basketball coach Chris Faulkner

In his autobiography, the great trumpeter Miles Davis (1989) describes the recording sessions of his 1970 album *Bitches Brew*, an album heavily inspired by the rock 'n roll zeitgeist of the 60s with long tracks of frenzied, sonic energy: "What we did on *Bitches Brew* you couldn't ever write down for an orchestra to play. That's why I didn't write it all out, not because I didn't know what I wanted; I knew that what I wanted would come out of a process and not some prearranged shit. This session was about improvisation, and that's what makes jazz so fabulous" (300).[1] Davis's strong nod toward improvisation over scripted performance recognizes a hallmark of jazz and illustrates the creative, collaborative freedom of jazz. During moments of improvisation, the soloist is simultaneously alone with notes and an instrument yet most commonly a part of a quartet or quintet playing before a live audience. At once, the solo is fluid and capricious yet woven into a tight tapestry of chords and melodies and harmonies. At once, the solo is flowing effortlessly, yet the

DOI: 10.7330/9781607326892.c005

soloist's body exerts itself greatly, fingers flying across an instrument, the bounce and tap of the foot in time to the rhythm section. As I quoted in the epigraph, jazz's emphasis on collaboration and bodily movement to an unfolding text leads James Lincoln Collier (1993) to draw parallels between jazz and athletics. Like athletics, jazz is embodied action in which a body in tandem with an instrument delivers written text and in which this textual delivery is directly reliant on the physical capabilities of the body. Both athletics and jazz capture mind-body collaborative creation in ever-changing circumstances.

The previous chapter articulates four ways to ensure that the material circumstances in which we work with student-athlete writers allow for sound pedagogy and practice. Building on that chapter, this final chapter contributes an answer to the question embedded in the title of chapters 3 and 4, a question many of us routinely ask but find little research addressing: how do we better teach our student-athlete writers? Two strands of research inform my answer: my own research into the men's basketball team at the University of North Georgia, covered in chapter 3, and jazz improvisation. For the former, I examined how student-athletes learn scripted plays based on my year-long immersion into the men's basketball team at UNG. I found players learn scripted plays through three cognitive processes: spatial orientation, haptic communication, and scaffolded situations. These processes theorize bodily reaction to an unfolding text. Moreover, these processes can find their way into our writing classes as theories of writing pedagogy. However, writing teachers cannot facilitate these processes the way a basketball coach can. I cannot ask the writer to run physically through drills; I cannot take the writer by the shoulder and spin them around or pivot their waist into a desired position like UNG's men's head basketball coach Chris Faulkner does with his players. We need pedagogical practices operating in the constraints and affordances of our curricular writing spaces. To sketch some practices onto which we can hang the cognitive processes of spatial orientation, haptic communication, and scaffolded situations, I turn to the second strand of research: jazz improvisation. Like athletics, this creative, collaborative, and performative art form relies on bodily reaction to an unfolding text. Recent work across diverse fields such as business, clinical psychology, writing center studies, and ethnomusicology chart the cognitive processes undergirding jazz—particularly improvisational soloing—and offer application to other creative learning organizations such as teacher-training programs and writing center tutoring and administration.[2]

The classroom and court are markedly different spaces. Nevertheless, through establishing a curricular atmosphere allowing for and helping student-writers toward improvisation (and the creative, collaborative, and embodied skills therein), we move closer to teaching our student-athletes based on their prior knowledge. I draw attention to prior knowledge here and more directly engage with it later in this chapter because of the importance writing-related transfer researchers such as Kathleen Blake Yancey, Liane Robertson, and Kara Taczak (Yancey, Robertson, and Taczak 2014) place on knowledge learners bring to new cognitive challenges. We must tap into student-athletes' prior knowledge, a knowledge largely informed by their often decade-long successful immersion into the bodily literacy of their sport, if we want our student-athlete writers to transfer explicitly and successfully the knowledge and practice honed in our writing classes to future writing contexts. In other words, if we strive toward the explicit transfer of writing knowledge and practice for our student-athlete writers—as we should for all our students—then we must understand the first three chapters of this book; we must understand how our student-athletes *already* engage with text, *already* write and perform text, *already* know text. We connect with this prior knowledge during curricular writing instruction through pedagogies harmonizing with this prior knowledge. Thus my attention to jazz in this final chapter.

Jazz improvisation happens in a cycle, a fixed-form foundation laid first by the rhythm section and then the harmony. The rhythm section—often the bass and drums—sets a fixed chord progression, and the soloist places moments of improvisational beauty gently on top of the rhythm. The soloist plays on top of the fixed layer. Without descending too deeply into music theory, to blow a solo fitting with a rhythm changing from number to number, the soloist works within a tight structure such as the twelve-bar or thirty-two-bar AABA. Within this structure, improvising can be a variance on a common melody or modal or harmonic improvising. In *Thinking in Jazz: The Infinite Art of Improvisation*, ethnomusicologist Paul F. Berliner (1994) constructs one of the more capacious discussions of this sonic performance delivered by the musician "spontaneously and intuitively" (2). In his section "Cultivating the Soloist's Skills," Berliner describes a soloist's training: "They formulate melodies by ear, kinetically (by hand), and through abstract visualization in relation to the sounds of each piece's underlying harmony" (159). This mind-body fusion drives thinking in jazz—to riff on Berliner's title—and facilitates the learning and performance of improvising. He writes, "The ideas that soloists realize during performance depend as much on the body's own actions as on the body's synchronous response to the mind. The body can take momentary control over particular activities . . . while the mind shifts its focus to the next ideas" (190). Because of the importance of the body and mind sharing tasks during cognitive performance, many musicians go to great physical lengths to train, modify, or alter their bodies for performance: training in dance and yoga, practicing relaxation techniques, regulating diet, imbibing drugs. Berliner writes of one trumpeter who asked a dentist to file down and "slightly separate his own front teeth in the hope that this would 'free up' his air stream" (Berliner, 1994, 119).

Scholars across a wide range of disciplines have molded jazz improvisation into a springboard for harnessing productivity in organizations, largely because of jazz's emphasis on collaborative, bodily creativity. Keith Sawyer (2004a; 2004b) looks to jazz as a model of creative improvisation to implement in teaching. Avoiding the common performance metaphor directed at teaching, which Sawyer believes carries connotations of tightly scripted and planned instruction focused on the teacher more than on the audience (i.e., the students), he describes a method of creative teaching grounded in "improvisational performance" (Sawyer 2004a, 12). Sawyer argues this method leads to "brighter, more motivated, and more effective teachers" and students with "deeper understanding and improved creative and social skills" (18). Frank Barrett (1998) also thinks more capaciously about jazz and suggests jazz improvisation carries seven characteristics transferable to any learning organization, not just the classroom.

1. Provocative competence: Deliberate efforts to interrupt habit patterns;

2. Embracing errors as a source of learning;

3. Shared orientation toward minimal structures that allow maximum flexibility;

4. Distributed task: continual negotiation and dialogue toward dynamic synchronization;

5. Reliance on retrospective sense-making;

6. "Hanging-out": Membership in a community of practice;

7. Taking turns soloing and supporting (606).

Elizabeth H. Boquet continues her interest in writing and music begun in *Noise from the Writing Center* in her coauthored chapter with Michele Eodice (Boquet and Eodice 2008). In "Creativity in the Writing Center: A Terrifying Conundrum," the lead chapter in the edited collection *Creative Approaches to Writing Center Work*, they take up Barrett's seven principles and place them in conversation with writing center work. They start with the premise that the everyday work of a writing center "requires" creativity (4) and then turn to Barrett's seven principles as a concrete framework onto which writing center tutors and administrators can construct creative ways for working with writers and running a writing center. For example, they begin with the first of Barrett's characteristics, which he titles "provocative competence" and explains as "deliberate efforts to interrupt habit patterns" (1998, 606). Boquet and Eodice argue, "Cruising on autopilot . . . thwarts meta-analysis and risk taking, requisite conditions for advancing creative approaches to learning" (8–9) and then turn to examples of tutor training that work to disrupt rote methods for working with writers. As with Sawyer and Barrett, Boquet and Eodice do not emphasize the music of jazz per se. Instead, they emphasize the essence of jazz, the creative, collaborative environment in which jazz is learned and performed and how such an environment can and should be replicated in other organizations where creativity fuels collaboratively driven activity. I turn to Barrett's characteristics and place them in harmony with the three cognitive processes student-athletes use to learn scripted plays from chapter 3. I do so because this harmonious coupling understands writing filtered through how our student-athletes know.[3] I see these cognitive processes as just that—models for learning located in one's head, which don't always lead to embodied action (for how often does it happen a player may *know* what to do on the court but fail to make that pass, take that shot, or run that route?). Cognitive processes form Barrett's characteristics and provide springboards to praxis.

In this chapter, I argue that the cognitive processes of spatial orientation, haptic communication, and scaffolded situations undergird the learning of scripted plays, but the embodied enactment of these plays is analogous to the characteristics of jazz improvisation Barrett extends to learning organization and Boquet and Eodice extend to working with writers. Learning scripted plays looks a whole lot like the jazzy, creative, and collaborative model of learning extended to various organizations.

Instead of walking through each of Barrett's seven characteristics, I draw attention to three I found prominent based on my work with the UNG men's basketball team. The first two are shared orientation toward minimal structures that allow maximum flexibility, and distributed task: continual negotiation and dialogue toward dynamic synchronization. I fold these two into the seventh characteristic, taking turns soloing and supporting. The student-athlete and coach voices heard in chapter 3 are heard again, but I ask readers to hear them anew. I ask readers to hear these voices as representative of all our students. In the fall 2017 semester, roughly 20.4 million students were expected to enroll in US higher education according to the *Digest of Education Statistics* compiled by the National Center for Education Statistics (National Center for Education Statistics 2017). If we work with the NCAA's report that 491,930 student-athletes competed in 2017–2018, then of these 20.4 million total students, roughly 2.5 percent were student-athletes. I write with the awareness that many readers may not work with student-athletes. Our two-year and open-admissions colleges, in particular, are rarely associated with college sports, and, as Holly Hassel and Joanne Baird Giordano (Hassel and Giordano 2013) remind us, the majority of our teaching and working with student-writers occurs at these schools. But student-athletes are not the only subgroup of our 20.2 million students who use bodily, athletic literacies. Over half our incoming college students self-reported as "Very much" (41 percent) or "Quite a bit" (13 percent) involved with "Athletic teams"; only a quarter self-reported as "Not at all" involved (Indiana University Bloomington Center for Postsecondary Research 2015). Eighty percent of our students visit the rec center weekly or play intramurals (Forrester 2014). If we work with the NCES's number of 20.4 million students, then 8 million were "very much" involved in high-school sports, and 16 million visit the rec center weekly or play intramurals. More than just 2.5 percent of our students know and learn through their bodies.

In my writing classes, I worked with a high-ranking Tai Kwon Do practitioner, a ballerina, the founder of the campus improvisational comedy troupe, a champion dragon boat paddler, and a former high-school volleyball star who, because of a knee injury, now volunteers as a high-school coach. The voices of some of those students appear in this chapter. I align them with the voices from chapter 3 and listen to these collective voices as the voices of our many many students who interact with text through their bodies. These voices have much to teach us about student writing.

At the risk of disappointing a reader, in the spirit of jazz music and college sports I do not conclude by offering a pedagogical template transportable to all learning contexts. For one, I have long been uncomfortable with the recipe-swapping tendency of composition studies when it comes to pedagogical practices, a tendency Paul Lynch (2013) extensively critiques in *After Pedagogy*.[4] In addition, a step-by-step approach to teaching such a creative process would surely cause Miles Davis to shriek from the grave, as he did not have patience for "prearranged shit." Both college sports and jazz articulate frameworks for learning and revolt against staid dictums and codified approaches. As Faulkner told me, "As far as on the court, we give them a framework as to how to play and let them play within that. We are not where you have to stand here, you gotta do this, you gotta do that." Instead of telling readers where to stand and what to do, I pose questions to help think about student-athlete writing instruction at the macro- (e.g., curricular development and writing program assessment) and microlevels (e.g., class objectives, assignments, activities). More specifically, these questions speak to the material circumstances of working with student-athlete writers. As I argue in chapter 4, before we sit and work with our student-athlete writers, we must ensure we have created an environment that does not harshly bifurcate the classroom and the court, an environment adhering to importance NCAA academic mandates and local athletics-department compliance statements while also incorporating best practices in teaching and learning coming out of the broad Scholarship of Teaching and Learning research and specific composition studies research. The questions in this chapter, then, do not advise on constructing syllabi or writing assignments but on how to think about the space we create with and for our student-athletes for delivering syllabi, for delivering writing assignments. I'm aware I'm addressing the question in the title of this chapter with a set of questions. Nevertheless, these questions-as-a-heuristic capture the essence of jazzy, creative, collaborative learning, a way of learning founded on shared principles but manifesting its sonic and embodied experience in countless ways.

I do, however, briefly nod to what I am currently doing in an FYC class where twenty-five of the twenty-six students are student-athletes. As I draft the final version of the book, we are only three weeks into the semester, and this is the first time I have had the opportunity to teach a class with such a large group of student-athletes. Near the end of this chapter, I describe a specific activity I used that is supported by recent research on teaching for writing-related transfer. But, returning to my previous argument, I offer this activity not as an activity that can be dug up and replanted for success elsewhere but as an activity growing out of my local context and responsive to research on student-athletes and transfer.

SHARED ORIENTATION: BALANCING MANIPULATION WITH A "FREELANCE TYPE OF THING"

In his early work on jazz improvisation and creativity, Keith Sawyer (1992) draws attention to the paradox driving jazz, what he describes as "the parallel tensions between conscious/nonconscious and structured/ innovative performance" (260). Writing in the journal *Organization Science*, Frank Barrett captures this paradox in his third characteristic transferable from jazz to any learning organization: "shared orientation toward minimal structures that allow maximum flexibility" (606). Great jazz exists on the border between a structured quintet and a capricious soloist. In his autobiography, Miles Davis (1989) writes about the composition of "I Wants to Stay Here (I Loves you, Porgy)" recorded in collaboration with composer Gil Evans. Davis explains, "He [Evans] wrote an arrangement for me to play on 'I Loves You, Porgy' and he wrote a scale I was supposed to play. No chords. He had used two chords for the other voicing, and so my passage of scales with those two chords gives you a lot of freedom and space to hear things" (230). Evans provided Davis a structure—albeit a minimal one—and Davis let loose his muted trumpet to roam freely atop this structure.

So too in college sports. And so too with how our student-athletes learn and embody scripted plays. Faulkner described to me his overall coaching philosophy during a long bus ride to an away game. As I wrote in the third chapter, Faulkner told me, "I can't tell you exactly what is going to happen [when my players run a play]. . . . Well, obviously, there are set plays where everything is manipulated, but most of the time it is a freelance type of thing." Faulkner teaches this balance through providing a clear framework and then allowing and even encouraging his players to deviate from and within this framework. Such a balance is challenging for many players. Faulkner told me early in the season that Sean Brennan, who had just transferred onto the team, constantly looked to Faulkner for more direction. Faulkner said, "I've even said to [Brennan], I've said, 'Brennan, I am not going to tell you you have to pass here.'" Faulkner and his coaching staff also surprised the team one practice with an odd offensive formation and instructions to guard against this formation. The players hesitantly milled around much to the frustration of assistant coach Richard Simmons, who wanted to provide more direction. But the players eventually aligned themselves into an effective defensive formation.

Faulkner prowls the sidelines during games and practices without a physical playbook full of scripted plays. Senior guard Travis Core found the lack of a playbook freeing. He even said a playbook would make the team "robotic" in that they would run the play exactly as scripted without concern for the many variables a team encounters: the defensive arrangement of the opposition, the rowdiness of the fans, the bend of the basketball rim, the feel of the gym floor, the time left on the clock, the score of the game. All these constraints influence how a team performs and encourage a jazzy approach to the game, which depends on spontaneous and collaborative action on top of a structured plan.

Paul Berliner (1994) provides an antecdote about the tempestuous bassist Charles Mingus upbraiding a promising young saxophonist while the two were before an audience. "Play something different, man; play something different," Mingus is quoted as saying. "This is jazz, man. You played that last night and the night before" (271). Core offered a similar anecdote about Faulkner: "I know he yells at us sometimes for running the play robotically," he told me. Core looks to scripted plays just like a jazz musician may look at notes—a push in a general direction without a constrictive predetermined outcome dictating all future embodied action. Core said plays "are designed to set you up to be successful, but if you break away from the play a little bit and do something really good that is better than running the play in general."

Our student-athletes balance this scripted/spontaneous paradox. Working with writers who know and learn text through bodily interaction invites us to consider how to construct with them a framework guiding how we work with writing and writers. And remembering the lessons of chapter 3, we would also do well to construct with them an atmosphere that encourages writers to understand when and how to work against this framework. Specifically, at the macro- and microlevels of writing instruction we should ask ourselves, *how can we create a space where our action and work with writers is grounded in discernable, understood, and accepted structures but made manifest in ways that allow flexibility and acknowledgment of the individual writer's agency?*

Again, I don't answer this question because the institutional, departmental, and classroom context mightily shapes responses to this *how* question. But an answer to this question should inform multiple levels of a writing program: curriculum design and assessment, individual freewriting at the beginning of class, activities funneling toward a major assignment, peer review. To be sure, many writing textbooks, writing assignments, conference talks, syllabi, and TA-training curricula allow leeway for improvisation—as one reviewer pointed out after reading a draft of this chapter. But the problem is that many student-athletes, like many students in general, don't take advantage of this leeway. Instead, these student-athletes find themselves cognitively floating, desperately wanted to anchor their floating thoughts to specific teacher directives. And here is where I return to my subargument in this chapter that these italicized questions invite us to design a space for improvisation that does not harshly bifurcate the classroom and the court. For many student-athletes I have worked with, the court or field is a space for free-flowing bodily creativity, creativity, of course, aligned with the larger structural team goals. The classroom, on the other hand, is not such a space. As Cheville (2001) found following her two-year study of the women's basketball team at Iowa, "Conceptual orientation central to knowledge acquisition in sport was relatively useless in college class-rooms that disassociated cognition from concrete activity and interaction" (8). This succinct and damning statement illustrates the need for writing instructors to design this space explicitly and consciously for all their learners.

Bodily spontaneity in jazz and athletics works because of the scripted action—be it musical notes or a hastily sketched basketball play—onto which the spontaneity occurs. But the spontaneity also works because our student-athletes, like jazz musicians, place their bodies in sync with those around them and take turns soloing and supporting.

DYNAMIC SYNCHRONIZATION AND TAKING TURNS SOLOING AND SUPPORTING: "'OH, CRAP, I GOTTA SET A SCREEN FOR THEM"

It was a late October afternoon. Six-feet-eight-inch junior forward T. J. Williams sat across from me in my office, his large frame folded tightly into the small leather chair. He was dressed in blue-and-gray UNG athletic wear, scratching his head with one hand and gripping his iPhone with the other. He had just finished practice about fifteen minutes earlier and beads of perspiration dotted his forehead. We talked about basketball plays and what he does if he forgets how to run a play during a game. Though Williams was the only player on the team who used a physical playbook in high school, he doesn't rely on mental visualization of scripted plays to trigger his memory. Instead, he remembers where to run, spin, and turn based on his coordinated movement with others. The majority of Williams's work on offense is setting screens for his teammates. By strategically placing his body in the path of a defender, he can free up his teammate for just enough time that his teammate can get an open shot or open pass. Williams told me that if he forgets a play, he quickly scans his immediate surroundings to see who near him is waiting for a screen. Williams says, "If someone is near me I will be like 'Oh, crap, I gotta set a screen for them.'" Williams echoes Faulkner's statement that "the most athletic guys learn by doing." This *doing* is a collaborative bodily interaction with others on the court. In the words of Barrett (1998), basketball teams strive toward "dynamic synchronization." In addition, in Barrett's words, "distributed task" and "continual negotiation" facilitate this synchronization. In chapter 3, I assert that haptic communication and spatial orientation facilitate student-athlete learning. Here I offer a more concrete practice: student-athletes, like jazz musicians, use touch and feel to rely on the continual coordination of their bodies with others. Touch and feel facilitate the ultimate goal of dynamic synchronization. Furthermore, players achieve dynamic synchronization through Barrett's seventh characteristic: taking turns soloing and supporting.

In *Jazz*, Gary Giddens and Scott DeVeaux break down Miles Davis's well-known opening number from his 1959 album *Kind of Blue* (Giddens and DeVeaux 2009). In the nine-minute-long "So What," Davis, John Coltrane, and Cannonball Adderley take turns leading solos supported by Jimmy Cobb on drums, Paul Chambers on bass, and Bill Evans on piano. Not only does the rhythm section support the soloist but so does the previous solo and the solo to come. Their musical movements are coordinated with those before, during, and after them—with those around them. According to Giddens and DeVeaux's analysis, Davis "plays short, concise phrases, *leaving ample space* for the rhythm section" at the 1:45 mark (422; emphasis added). At the 3:38 mark, Coltrane "switches to a more intense style of improvising. . . . Evans *responds* with a peculiar composing pattern" (423; emphasis added). Adderley enters around the fifth minute. The rhythm section quiets down, and Adderley enters "*mimicking* Coltrane's extensive double-bass lines" (423; emphasis added). By 1959, Davis and Coltrane were both stars in their own right. Davis had kicked his heroin addiction, which he had seen kill Charlie Parker in 1955 and Billie Holiday just months before Davis recorded *Kind of Blue*. Davis also found himself at the forefront of a new jazz subgenre: hard bop. Coltrane released the highly regarded album *Blue Train* and was a few short years away from recording his masterpiece *A Love Supreme*. Despite their musical prominence, Davis and Coltrane needed each other and the rest of the ensemble for this track, thus the emphasis I placed on the collaboratively focused verbs in Giddens and DeVeaux's reading. Davis (1989) writes in his autobiography that he "didn't write out the music for *Kind of Blue* . . . because I wanted a lot of spontaneity in the playing" (234). The spontaneity sought by Davis could only be captured by give and take and continual negotiation toward dynamic synchronization. The synchronization among musicians continues for another four minutes in "So What" until Evans's keys are the only sound. And then they too fall silent, and thus ends one of the more well-known, critically renowned, and commercially popular modal jazz songs.

Like jazz quintets, basketball teams direct individual talents toward a collective goal. Sean Brennan was a first-year player the year I followed the team. He transferred from a Division I school in Florida and worked his way into the starting lineup for the Nighthawks. And he took a teammate's position. For the previous three years, Core had run point guard and directed the action on the court, acting as a liaison between his teammates and coach. Now, because Core was a fourth-year senior and leader of the team, Faulkner asked Core to change positions to accommodate Brennan's talents. Core moved to shooting guard. Core's job as shooting guard is to support Brennan's work as point guard and to adjust rapidly to any change Brennan makes to a play. Barrett (1998) writes that taking turns soloing and supporting asks a musician to "see beyond the player's current vision, perhaps provoking the soloist in [a] different direction" (617). Travis gives a similar visual description of his new role: "Because I am usually seeing it from the one [the point-guard position] and then when he [Brennan] calls the play I am like 'uh' and then I am 'Okay, there we go.'"

Paul Berliner writes of the ever-changing landscape of group dynamics within jazz improvisation, a landscape remarkably similar to the one Core traverses on the court:

> Without warning . . . anyone in the group can suddenly take the music in a direction that defies expectation, requiring the others to make instant decisions as to the development of their own parts. When pausing to consider an option or take a rest, the musician's impression is of a "great rush of sounds" passing by, and the player must have the presence of mind to track its precise course before adding his or her powers of musical invention to the group's performance. Every maneuver or response by an improviser leaves its momentary trace in the music. By journey's end, the group has fashioned a composition anew, an original product of their interaction (Berliner 1994, 349)

Both Berliner's descriptive argument and Davis's track "So What" illustrate a slight disconnect between jazz and basketball worth noting. Berliner writes of a "fashioned composition," a finished product for the sonic appreciation of the listeners. With the track "So What," listeners hear a polished version of dynamic synchronization. Williams and Core offer a behind-the-scenes look at the messy process of placing others in sync with a common directive. To alleviate this messiness, student-athletes work in tandem with each other and coaches, constantly dialoging and negotiating and distributing the work. Early in the season, Faulkner worked his team through foundational offensive plays. When something went awry, Faulkner walked to Shaquan Cantrell, took him by the elbow, moved him around, and said "I don't think we need to screen him [the defender]. I think we can just cut." Core suggested a similar adjustment to a different play, and Faulkner nodded approval. Then the action began again. Here the harsh delineation between coach and player is flattened as both share the work of bettering team synchroniza-tion. Coach and player fused momentarily into a singular role, offering adjustments to a script based on physical movement.

This principle dovetails with Barret's (1998) principle of flexibility with minimal structures. For our student-athletes to work toward collabora-tive, bodily movement, they need the flexibility to amend, modify, delete, or add to the current text—just as Faulkner allowed Core. Through dia-logue and shared responsibility, the team is able to run a scripted play fluidly in a game. As Core told me, "It is more muscle-memory-it. You hear the play, and it triggers something in you and you go."

Our student-athletes, like jazz musicians, share the tasks necessary for collective and dynamic synchronization with their teammates. Sometimes these tasks ask for a renegotiation of the responsibilities, as when Core suggested an amendment to a play. Sometimes these tasks ask for a redefinition of responsibilities, as when Core moved from the point-guard positon to the shooting-guard position to make room for Brennan's talents. But ultimately, these tasks involve coordinated bodily meaning making with others—as Williams demonstrates with his incessant quest to screen somebody. Working with writers who know and learn text through bodily dynamics with others invites us to consider how to construct a framework for writers and writing reli-ant on the voices of others and on knowing when to let others' voices speak before, instead of, or after our own. Specifically, we should ask two questions:

- *How can we create a space for our students to understand that their written actions are always already caught in a web of relations so that one plucked string vibrates all others, so that one movement impacts a teammate, so that one sentence influences another's voice?*

- *How can we create a space for students to understand that while their name may be in the upper-left hand corner, at times they need to recede and let others speak, let others play, let others shoot?*

The questions I pose are not asking us to reapproach writing radically and, if they are stripped of the athletic and jazz imagery, are found in many composition pedagogy books. The first, for example, draws on readings from Elizabeth Wardle and Doug Downs's second edition of *Writing about Writing*, which I use in my FYC classes, specifically selections on activity theory (Wardle and Downs 2014). In the second edition of *Rewriting: How to Do Things with Texts,* Joseph Harris (2006) describes a similar framework in which student writers see their voices as part of a larger conversation. Harris draws from Kenneth Burke's (1973) well-known example of arriving late to a discussion at a parlor, taking time to listen to the ebb and flow of conversation, and then entering one's metaphorical oar into the waters of the conversation. By positioning academic writing as a conversation, Harris introduces the idea of writing as "recirculating," in which a writer "highlights parts of [the] text for the consideration of others" (36), and writing as an act of "forwarding" that "tak[es] words, images, or ideas from [texts] and put[s] them in new contexts" (37). In sum, Harris offers up writing as a collaborative, social enterprise. I submit that Harris's recirculating is a form of collaboration much like the kind central to improvisation in jazz and basketball because of how multiple bodies develop a structure and facilitate meaning making. What is missing in Harris's text is an emphasis on living, breathing bodies central to collaboration as recirculation. He elides an emphasis on the materiality of writers.

In *The Open Hand: Arguing as an Art of Peace*, Barry Kroll (2013) recognizes the physical body. Like Harris, Kroll views writing as a collaboratively grounded activity, but he does not think of forwarding and recirculating—to borrow Harris's gerunds—as just conceptual activities; Kroll communicates a physical dimension to writing as a collaborative, social enterprise. Through introducing his students to the Japanese martial-arts form aikido, in which practitioners redirect the energy of their opponents, Kroll asks students to literally feel the physical movements of their opponents and carry this physical action into conceptual expository argument. Reflecting on aikido in the writing class, Kroll writes, "I found an especially receptive audience among student athletes, who were eager to use their bodily intelligence in an academic course" (12). Though Harris's and Kroll's views of writing align a great deal with the collaborative, bodily activity of jazz and athletics, I hold that the athletic and jazz imagery in my italicized questions—really imagery grounded in creative, collaborative bodily activity—is what makes these questions stand apart and is more apt for working with student-athlete writers, or any student who thinks through their body, than what is in our current scholarship. These questions also attempt to tap into students' prior knowledge. Kroll gets close to thinking directly about prior knowledge when he reflects on how receptive student athletes are to his unique pedagogical activities. We need to get closer. We now know of prior knowledge's centrality for engaging with new or challenging cognitive tasks. The struggles we encounter with student-athlete writers—or any writer for that matter—may be ameliorated by explicitly connecting their athletic prior knowledge to new curricular cognitive activities.

STUDENT-ATHLETES AND PRIOR KNOWLEDGE

In *Writing across Contexts: Transfer, Composition, and Sites of Writing,* Yancey, Robertson, and Taczak (2014) draw from the National Research Council's volume *How People Learn: Mind, Brain, Experience, and School* (Bransford, Pellegrino, and Donovan 2000). According to this volume, all "new learning involves transfer based on previous learning" (5). Using *How People Learn* as a springboard to consider writing-related transfer, Yancey, Robertson, and Taczak, too, argue for the centrality of prior knowledge. They declare early in their book that prior knowledge is a pivotal cognitive block composers bring to writing and that it aids in successful transfer. They found that "prior knowledge—of various kinds—plays a decisive if not determining role in students' successful transfer of writing knowledge and practice" (5). This bold claim—I note *various* and *determining*—should startle readers, particularly those who construct an impenetrable wall between curricular and extracurricular writing. When I read this claim, my mind turned to the scores of student-athletes I talked with, the scores of student-athletes who huddled over a screen or piece of paper with me and pounded out word after word after word. The capaciousness of *various* leads me to the bodily literacy our student-athletes and many other students display outside our classrooms.

In their fourth chapter, "How Students Make Use of Prior Knowledge in the Transfer of Knowledge and Practice in Writing," Yancey, Robertson, and Taczak (2014) define transfer as "a dynamic activity through which students, like all composers, actively make use of prior knowledge as they respond to new writing tasks" (103). Onto this constructed definition, they erect an argument that prior knowledge can function in three ways: assemblage, remix, or setback (104). The third, I hold, resonates most strongly with student-athletes. They write, "An individual's prior knowledge—located in a community context—might be at odds with the requirements of a given writing situation" (105). Thus, just as researchers conceptualize and learners experience successful and unsuccessful transfer (not unsuccessful in the sense that transfer does not happen but in that what is transferred by the learners hinders the ability to complete the new cognitive task), researchers conceptualize and learners experience that, simply, "some prior knowledge provides help for new writing situations, while other prior knowledge does not" (Yancey, Robertson, and Taczak 2014, 105). A challenge remaining, and one I end on here, is how to develop a writing class allowing for our student-athletes' bodily prior knowledge to flourish and connect with new practices and knowledge of writing.

If we are honest with ourselves, this flourishing and connecting simply isn't happening in many of our classes. During my decade working with student-athlete writers, I have found that few student-athletes and instructors acknowledge or even consider connections between writing and athletics, connections between the classroom and the court or field. I recall talking with a first-year wide receiver at Auburn competing in his first season on the team and enrolled in FYC. He described how he runs his routes against a defender. He specifically talked about watching how his opponent moves and how he adjusts his route based on his opponent's movement. He also described how, after he runs past an opponent, he attempts to, in his words, "restack," or ensure he is running directly in front of and not to the side of his opponent. I remember thinking how similar these bodily movements are to the rhetorical moves we make as writers in anticipation of and reaction to potential or realized counterarguments; however, I struggled with helping the student-athlete see these connections. I am aware that, as the old adage goes, the plural of *anecdote* is not *data*. Yet my anecdote coupled with Julie Cheville's (2001) research leads me to argue we have much more work to do to connect with athletic prior literacy in our writing classes. Her findings lead her to assert that the "conceptual orientation central to knowledge acquisition in sport was relatively useless in college classrooms that disassociated cognition from concrete activity and interaction" (8). Such a powerful assertion backed by years of research is unsettling indeed. In my writing classes, I attempt to connect with students' prior athletic literacy with mixed results. In the following section, I start with a story of failure and one of success and then describe a writing assignment I am using in a section of FYC where twenty-five of the twenty-six students enrolled are student-athletes.

The story of failure: the year after I followed the men's basketball team, the assistant coach called me up. He asked me to come to his office and chat about one of their incoming first-year players. The player was not a highly touted recruit with thousands of followers on Instagram and the media attention of ESPNU. But the player had come to our school with some academic and life challenges. The assistant coach asked me to work with the player, and the player enrolled in my 8 a.m. FYC class. The player—let's call him Kris—was quiet, reserved. He always made it to this early class, his hoodie pulled over his head and his eyes asking for just a few more hours of sleep. In other words, he was just like most of the other twenty students in the class. He struggled mightily with writing. Again, like most students, he could pull off a quick five-paragraph essay and trick an automated scoring machine into giving him a solid mark. However, to use Joseph Harris's (2006) language, Kris struggled with recirculating and forwarding. For Kris, as for many other student writers, connecting with the voice of others proved challenging. In one assignment taken from our class textbook (the second edition of Elizabeth Wardle and Doug Downs's *Writing about Writing* [Wardle and Downs 2014]), I asked students to perform a rhetorical analysis of a previous writing assignment they had completed. In preparation, we read Keith Grant-Davie's (1997) "Rhetorical Situations and Their Constituents," and I asked students to use Grant-Davie as a lens for viewing and then reflecting on how they invented, drafted, and edited a previous paper. Kris analyzed a paper he wrote his senior year in high school and was able to sprinkle in many specific details about his writing experience. But the Grant-Davie reading was missing. It was as if the reading we did in class fulfilled one activity and writing the paper fulfilled another. As the teacher, I saw the reading and the writing as a metaphorical estuary where the two converged into a newly formed creation. Kris did not. We chatted briefly during class and in my office about implementing the ideas of others into one's own writing. Ultimately, I did not help him see his final paper as this estuary and not a mountain range harshly cutting off one landscape, one cognitive activity, from another.

Though I taught Kris for two sections of FYC, I feel I let him down in that he left my class after a full academic year and never understood that what he wanted and needed to say was part of a larger conversation. Kris is not unique. Other student writers, even seasoned academic writers, are often asked to dig deeper into the literature, read this article, cite this very important book. What makes Kris a unique case, however, is that his struggles with recirculating are similar to his struggles with recirculating in basketball, his most successful writing space. Kris struggled because of prior knowledge—or, really, a lack of it.

When I attended basketball practices, I watched Kris fly around the gym, his long arms causing a nuisance on defense, his long legs flying him down the court on offense. But now that I think back to those practices, Kris took to the court as he took to his writing: alone, detached from those around him, not intentionally uniting himself to the ongoing action around him. The head coach agreed when I chatted with him about Kris's academic performance. Our conversation led to Kris's struggle adjusting to college ball. *Maybe,* I wondered silently to myself, *Kris could not see his writing as a collaborative, bodily activity because his extracurricular prior literacy, a literacy foundational to who Kris is, wasn't either.* He did not have prior knowledge of recirculation to draw upon when he entered my classroom every Tuesday and Thursday morning for an entire academic year.

Kris is no longer at the University of North Georgia. Like the first student-athlete I worked with closely at Auburn, and who opened and will soon close this book, Kris is gone.

Now the story of success: I have found traction in inviting students to see writing as a collaborative, bodily activity—much like athletics. I have specifically asked students to use freewriting to explore some ideas about collaboration in the sport they currently play or did play.

One student wrote in regards to her experience with dragon-boat racing, a team paddle sport. Her experience culminated in her team's winning the overall Nation's Cup at the International Canoe Federation Dragon Boat World Championships in Poland.

> With dragon boat we also had [to] work as a unified team, the more unified that the team was the better in cadence the team was with the drummer but the drummer was not the person setting the cadence, the two lead strokes are the people who sets the cadence, everyone is supposed to follow the person in front of themselves the drummer just helps so that everyone can stay in perfect cadence.

Another student described the coordinated effort of learning a gymnastics routine.

> For the younger girls, they learn the routine at the same time and practice together with multiple girls doing the routine at the same time so they get the hang of it. Once they get it down . . . they perform individually. They/ we learn it by our coaches telling and showing us what to do, and by repetition and fixing our corrections.

Both these excerpts directly engage with collaboration as central to learning and performing bodily activities. Dragon boat paddling, like paddling a two-person kayak or rowing a racing shell, depends on synchronized bodily action. Each roughly six-hundred-pound boat—plus the weight of twenty-two other people—typically has twenty paddlers sitting in two parallel rows. To drive the massive boat forward, paddlers not only ensure that all twenty paddles enter and leave the water at the same time but also that the paddles enter near the thigh of the person in front of them. Stretching forward with the paddle to the person in front ensures longer strokes, a faster boat. Even gymnastics, which is very much an individual sport, is founded on a principle of "multiple girls doing the routine at the same time so they get the hang of it," according to my student. Working together builds a structure for learning, but this structure is not the goal. For gymnastics, dragon-boat paddlers, basketball players, and student writers, the goal is to learn how to move with and against this structure. The goal is improvising.

We want our students to see writing as a collaborative, bodily activity giving birth to a structure. From this structure, we want our students to improvise, make the structure their own, see the structure as a guide and not an absolute. For jazz, this vague noun *structure* is commonly the twelve-bar or thirty-two-bar AABA. For basketball, this structure is a specific scripted play, and the improvisation is suddenly and rapidly adjusting the play ever so slightly during a game. For our writing classes, this structure is common genres like a literacy narrative, a research paper, a multimodal digital composition. And the improvisation is adjusting, modifying the genre to fix the ever-changing rhetorical situation.

Kris struggled with improvising because he didn't fit himself into the structure and position himself as a teammate coordinating a play with others. If he did try to improvise, it came across as aloofness, selfishness, chasing stats over wins. If a student-writer tries to improvise without knowing the structure, it comes across as not following directions, not reading the assignment sheet.

Our work as writing teachers impels us to introduce students to the structure undergirding the work in our classroom. This structure imbues our syllabus, handouts, assignments, activities, and assessment. Once we introduce our structure, we would do well to work with our student-writers to see how their prior knowledge grounded in their bodily extracurricular literacies might help them improvise with and against this structure. Drawing on students' prior knowledge of bodily literacy, we can move toward allowing the questions I posed in italics to guide macro- and micro-level work with student-athlete writers, which will help teachers and students of writing see the inextricable link between the body and writing and see connections between the classroom and the court in ways previously unacknowledged.

STUDENT-ATHLETES AND METACOGNITION

But tapping into our student-athletes' prior knowledge isn't enough. As a wealth of recent literature (e.g., national consensus documents, books, research reports, articles, and statements) has taught us in the past decade, writers need to think about their thinking in a structured fashion to facilitate successful writing-related transfer. This structured thinking about thinking is termed *reflection* or *metacognition*, certainly with important distinctions between the two but with the common emphasis on bettering future performance. The national consensus document *Framework for Success in Postsecondary Writing* (CWPA, NCTE, and NWP 2011) opts for the term *metacognition* when forwarding eight habits of mind that are "both intellectual and practical and that will support students' success in a variety of fields and disciplines" (1). The Elon Statement on Writing Transfer—developed by forty-five writing researchers who attended the Elon Research Seminar (ERS) from 2011 to 2013—stresses "students' meta-awareness . . . [and] reflective writing [which] promotes preparation for transfer and transfer-focused thinking" (Elon University 2013, 4). To enable writing transfer, the Elon Statement specifically suggests "asking students to engage in activities that foster the development of metacognitive awareness" (5). Published just one year after the ERS concluded, Yancey, Robertson, and Taczak's *Writing across Contexts* (2014) emphasizes structured and reiterative student reflection woven throughout their sixteen-week curriculum, which they term *teaching for transfer* and which was originally implemented at Florida State. In their appendices, they include the syllabus and the assignment sheets for the three major assignments. Yancey, Robertson, and Taczak opt for the term *reflection* instead of *metacognition*; for all three assignments, students compose a reflective paper in conjunction with the major assignment. Indeed, *reflection* is a key word for the course and one central to the theory of writing students eventually author at the end of the course. This theory of writing serves as a metaphorical passport allowing students to travel to various other writing contexts inside and outside higher education.

Yancey, Robertson, and Taczak (2014) offer one way to incorporate thinking about thinking smoothly into the construction of a curriculum. In *A Rhetoric of Reflection*, Yancey (2016) points out that reflection has a long history with composition studies, and individual contributions to this edited collection communicate more ways to conceptualize and teach students how to think about their thinking. Chris Anson and Jessie Moore's coedited *Critical Transitions: Writing and the Question of Transfer* (named, in part, after the ERS) includes a contribution by Gwen Gorzelsky, Dana Lynn Driscoll, Joe Paszek, Ed Jones, and Carol Hayes that provides a description of a taxonomy designed to teach what they call "constructive cognition" (Gorzelsky et al. 2017, 216). These sources do not exhaust recent conceptualizations of reflection in the writing classroom but illustrate that even as continued focus on thinking about thinking linked to transfer has spread out in multiple directions, the emphasis throughout has been that thinking about thinking supports transfer, that must be structured into a curriculum, and that must be explicitly taught.

Metacognition links up with the prior knowledge of our student-athletes. When I spent a year with the UNG men's basketball team, I sat in on film sessions head coach Chris Faulkner held in any empty classroom he could find. Assistant coach Josh Travis brought in a laptop and hooked it up to the classroom projector. The basketball players folded their large frames into the hard plastic desks. Some, too big for the desks, elected to sit on top and drape their legs over the side. With a dry-erase marker, Faulkner pointed to the action on the screen and periodically scribbled notes on the whiteboard. I sat in the back row as Faulkner taught, as he led his players through structured metacognition of their own physical and cognitive performances. He moved between talking about collective performance and individual performance, but the two were also coupled—much like a writer reflects on a single sentence on page 3 but reflects on how this single sentence contributes to the whole of the argument. If players reflected on their performance individually and on their own time, I wasn't privy to these moments, and none of the players I interviewed mentioned such moments. Reflection, instead, was a team event, structured into the curriculum of the season and directly tied to the larger team goal of bettering performance and winning games.

Because the team—and the entire UNG athletics department—worked with such meager financial resources, the film sessions took place wherever space was available. When on the UNG campus, Faulkner looked for an empty classroom. When traveling for an away game, Faulkner looked for any quiet space. When I traveled with the team to a game against Clayton State, Travis set the team up in a corner. He set his laptop on a hard, white plastic chair and set four other chairs in a semicircle around the laptop. High-dollar athletic programs make use of more opulent space, spaces that often look like movie theaters—a large screen in an auditorium with rows of leather recliners. But no matter whether the players are lounging in La-Z-Boys or rigid white plastic chairs, the goal for film sessions is again structured reflection directed toward the larger goals of the team.

In his contribution to *Naming What We Know: Threshold Concepts in Writing Studies*, Howard Tinberg (2015) asserts metacognition helps writers develop "the ability to perceive the very steps by which success occurs" (76) by helping writers in "discerning the structure of a draft; delineating patterns of error; or discriminating between what is necessary in a draft and what in the end serves little purpose" (78). So too does metacognition operate in sports if we substitute Tinberg's word *draft* with *play* or *movement*. With the focus on team success, film sessions ask players to focus collectively and individually on what worked, what didn't, and how they can continue folding their bodies into dynamic synchronization with those around them.

Here I think of that moment during the November practice I detail in chapter 3. Faulkner moved Shaquan Cantrell into a different bodily position within the scripted play. In the words of Tinberg (2015), the basketball team witnessed Faulkner discriminating between what "is necessary" and what "in the end serves little purpose" (78). How Cantrell originally positioned his hips served little purpose to the larger goal of the scripted play. By altering Cantrell's hip position—and telling the players why—Faulkner helped the team to, again in Tinberg's words, "perceive the very steps by which success occurs" (76). Faulkner's teaching and modeling of metacognition for his players was so effective it immediately spurred further reflection on the part of senior guard Travis Core, who suggested an amendment to an additional play. Core quickly considered the structure of the play he wanted to amend, noticed an error pattern (in this case the position of a body within the play), and thought a different bodily position could better serve the larger goal of the scripted play. Faulkner granted this amendment. And through this metacognitive process, scripted plays as text are born; like all text, they are not born in a vacuum but are tethered to their past, present, and future rhetorical contexts and amended or erased through the rhetor's reflecting on the past, present, and future performance of the text. Introducing structured reflective activities into our curriculums, such as those mentioned in *Writing across Contexts*, connects with student-athletes' prior knowledge of reflecting for their sport.

MOVING FORWARD WITH STUDENT-ATHLETES, JAZZ, AND TRANSFER . . .

In these final pages, it behooves me to ask a direct question: what is next regarding student-athletes, writing, and literacy? In tandem with the Association of American Colleges and Universities, George Kuh (2008) identifies first-year seminars and experiences, which include critical inquiry and frequent writing, and writing-intensive courses as high-impact educational practices. As higher education stakeholders, particularly university systems and boards of regents, implement initiatives that place a premium on retention and graduation, I join my voice with other writing-related-transfer researchers and teachers who forecast a dominant role for teaching for writing transfer. Therefore, and returning to the *what next?* query, we would do well to work closely with our student-athletes and leverage recent work on writing transfer, specifically the teaching-for-transfer (TFT) curriculum articulated in *Writing across Contexts*.

I've spent a decade working closely with student-athletes, thinking and reading about their writing practices, presenting on how and what they know, and advocating on their behalf at conferences and department meetings, on listservs, and in publications. I have even inserted slivers of my research on student-athlete literacy into my general sections of FYC—and I provide some of these slivers early in this chapter along with excerpts of student writing. But I had never allowed my research to form my entire semester-long curriculum. And I had never taught a class in which the majority of the students on the roll were student-athletes.

As I prepared to send the final draft of this book to Utah State University Press, I received permission from the UNG athletics department to do both. As I type these sentences, I am teaching a section of English 1102—the second step in UNG's two-step FYC sequence—in which twenty-five of the twenty-six students enrolled are student-athletes. It would be improper to have a class of just student-athletes; any class should be open to all enrolled students. The lone non-student-athlete in my class is enrolled not as a result of the UNG athletics department's cynically skirting the rules. Student-athletes at UNG, as at most other schools, have priority registration because of the need to schedule classes around morning and/or afternoon practices. Honors students and students with documented disabilities also have priority registration. Several months before the spring semester rolled around, I reached out to UNG's faculty athletics representative, who serves triple duty as the FAR, a math professor, and the only athletics advisor. She meets regularly with most of the student-athletes, particularly the ones academically struggling, and first- and second-year student-athletes. The FAR and I ensured that a class with mainly student-athletes did not constitute an NCAA compliance violation. She then promoted my Tuesday/Thursday 9:30 a.m. English 1102 class to the many student-athletes she advised. The class filled during the priority registration period. When I entered the class on the first day, the students had separated themselves into sports. All the men with the hats were at the middle table—the baseball players. Women's softball sat off to the left; women's soccer and cross-country merged together off to the right. One men's basketball player and one men's soccer player found empty desks.

In preparing to bring this curriculum to my work with student-athletes, I attended the full-day workshop Yancey, Robertson, Matt Davis, and Erin Workman led at the Council of Writing Program Administrators conference in Raleigh, North Carolina. I sat at a round table with smart, engaged, and committed attendees and, based on the material in the workshop, we worked though how to implement TFT at our institutions in response to our own varied local contexts. After the conference, Robertson graciously talked over the phone with me about nuances of the curriculum, and, in line with my administrative position as director of FYC, I led a series of workshops within my home department on TFT. Thanks to a grant from our Center for Teaching, Learning, and Leadership, I purchased ten copies of *Writing across Contexts* for my colleagues.

I write all this to support my assertion that this curriculum is strongly suited for working with student-athletes because of its emphasis on prior knowledge and metacognition. While it is too early in the semester for any definitive statements or qualitative or quantitative data about how this curriculum facilitates student-athlete writing development, I do describe an assignment.

We are using Elizabeth Wardle and Doug Downs's *Writing about Writing* (2014. The *WAW* curriculum drives more toward students' developing rhetorical awareness, while the TFT curriculum drives more toward student's developing rhetorical knowledge. But the readings in *Writing about Writing*, particularly the readings on rhetoric and on learners weaving extracurricular literacies into curricular ones, are particularly apt for helping student-athletes develop knowledge and practices of writing, which are grounded in their prior knowledge, facilitated by their metacognition, and designed to help them write across a wide variety of future contexts.

The TFT curriculum introduces students to eleven key terms; I adopted eight for my class: *genre, exigence, audience, rhetorical situation, reflection, context, discourse community,* and *knowledge.* The first four weeks of the semester drew students' attention to four of these terms. On the second day, I moved students through a quick presentation I designed on the cloud-based platform Slides.com titled Athletics & Writing. It is on the open-access class website (rifenburg1102.blogspot.com) and my own website (mrifenburg.wordpress.com). This slide presentation began with images I collected during my research, many of them found in the pages of this book: Auburn's defensive football play, a hand-drawn basketball play, head coach Chris Faulkner kneeling to draw a play during a time-out. I then drew commonalities between authoring a scripted play and authoring an academic paper. In drawing these commonalities, I specifically highlighted our first four key terms.

I then brought student's attention to the first of five writing assignments for the semester: a five hundred-word minipaper in which they pick one of the four key terms, explain how the term is defined in Keith Grant-Davie's "Rhetorical Situations and their Constituents"—found in

Writing about Writing—and then state how understanding this term will help them in future writing contexts, be these contexts academic or nonacademic. The focus in this brief writing assignment is to have students begin close readings of texts to define a term and then apply this definition to their own writing.

To scaffold this assignment, students worked in groups on the Grant-Davie reading. Collaboratively they answered a series of questions:

- What is Grant-Davie's most important point about exigence? About audience?

- Think about competing in a game for your sport. Who are the different kinds of audiences watching and responding to how you compete? What kinds of expectations do these audiences have for how you compete?

- Think about a paper you wrote for a class last semester. Now look at the three questions Grant-Davie asks about exigence on pages 352 and 353 (What is the discourse about? Why is the discourse needed? What is the discourse trying to accomplish?). Answer these three questions in regards to your previous paper.

As I rotated around, listening in on conversations, I was particularly struck by how the student-athletes thought through the second prompt about audience. The baseball players talked about scouts, umpires, and opposing coaches as audiences with different levels of expectations; the group of women soccer players talked of having parents and friends in the stands, both watching the game but watching with different needs and interests. Students then individually answered these prompts on a Google doc, which they placed in a folder they shared with me.

The initial question about defining terms directs relates to the mini-paper, the second calls upon student-athletes' prior knowledge about audience to begin to understand how Grant-Davie and those within composition studies understand audience, and the third question plants a seed for the second writing assignment, a fifteen hundred-word rhetorical analysis of a previous writing assignment taken from chapter 3 of *Writing about Writing*. Collectively, these questions tap into student-athletes' prior knowledge and ask student-athletes to reflect on how elements of the rhetorical situation—in this case, audience—is at play in text for their sport.

The audience question also inches students closer to seeing how effective writing—like jazz and like athletics—is not a fixed, full-in-the-template form of communication. Instead, it is responsive to underlying structures but also free flowing and responsive to ever-shifting rhetorical situations. For example, the baseball players talked of different kinds of audiences watching the game. A catcher may send a signal to a pitcher based on the expectation of one audience, say, the opposing hitter, and then send another signal based on the expectations of another audience, say, their own head coach. Sometimes the needs of these multiple audiences overlap but the ever-changing needs demand an ever-changing text. Just like in jazz. And just like in academic writing. That is what I need to show them before they can play along with others in writing.

I stressed to my students on the first day that the class is not about sports. We are not talking sports, reading articles about sports. Supported by Anne Beaufort's (2007) findings, Yancey, Robertson, and Taczak (2014) assert content matters and "contributes in very specific ways to students' intentional transfer of knowledge and practice in writing (61). As such, they warn against "too much 'floating' content— content unmoored to specific writing theory or practice" (88). Instead, we are explicitly connecting with the epistemologies of student-athletes, the ways of engaging, learning, and knowing scripted plays as text and implementing these texts in the ever-shifting rhetorical situation of athletic competition. College athletics demand that student-athletes bring their prior knowledge to sites of new learning; college athletics also demand that student-athletes reflect individually and collectively on past performance in hopes of bettering future performance. These two critical elements—prior knowledge and metacognition—are also central to TFT.

Though the semester has only just begun, I believe this curriculum is well suited for helping student-athletes develop writing skills transferable to future writing contexts. I have already uploaded the majority of the class writing assignments and activities to our class website and will post my own reflections of the course to my website and articulate some early findings in local newspaper Op-Eds, as I strongly believe in communicating my work to a public audience.

. . . BUT WITH A CHALLENGE

In one hand, I hold the importance of prior knowledge in my work with student-athlete writers. In the other hand, I hold Chris Anson's (2016) research pointing to the troubling nature of some prior knowledge, specifically his point regarding the "universal challenge of transfer regardless of prior experience" (519). Anson returns me to Kris, the first-year basketball player I taught and who left UNG after one rocky season. In Anson's case study of Martin, a successful academic writer roped into penning brief texts for the local newspaper about his son's Pop Warner football team, Anson illustrates that successfully writing in one setting does not always transfer to successfully writing in another. Martin struggled mightily over these brief game summaries, spending hours tinkering with the language and staring into the screen. Even when he finished writing, he noticed the newspaper editor and football team coordinator heavily edited his prose. The struggles continued for the whole season with Martin never able to match the seemingly capricious expectations of the editor and coordinator. When the season ended, his son did not play football again, and Martin (whom Anson identifies as himself near the end of the article) still finds himself puzzled by the challenge posed by these blurbs many years later. Anson draws from Hogan Hayes, Dana Ferris, and Carl Withaus's term "frustrated transfer" (Hayes et al. 2017 quoted in Anson 2016, 532) as a way to conceptualize the struggles encountered by a successful academic writer with writing in a new or unfamiliar setting. Anson's large point is to push against an easy nod toward seeing prior knowledge as a panacea for writers who struggle with transfer.

Via Anson, when we think about Kris, we cannot quickly point the finger toward prior knowledge and state he could not recirculate writing in FYC because he could not recirculate in basketball. We can say we are looking at a learner who struggles to situate himself within larger conversations and that here is a case in which the "conceptual orientation central to knowledge acquisition" (Cheville 2001, 8) in the *classroom* may inform the court or vice versa. Cheville argues that what is learned on the court does not mirror what is learned in the classroom. Here we may have a case in which the court informs the classroom, in which extracurricular literacies inform curricular ones. As I talked informally with the head basketball coach about Kris, I learned that on the court, as in the classroom, Kris approached a task alone. He took to the court with tunnel vision and struggled to see himself as a part of the team. Just as in his writing, he did not situate himself with the other bodies on the court, the other voices in the conversations. One cannot recirculate or even begin to improvise against a given structure without synchronizing with others.

As Anson argues, transfer is tough no matter the level of one's prior knowledge. Yet what happens when there is no prior knowledge to transfer? What happens when a writer cannot recirculate their writing because they cannot recirculate within one of their most successful areas of literate practice? Certainly one may pause at *successful* because Kris ultimately left the team; however, he represents the tiny percent of the high-school population who received a scholarship to play college ball. According to NCAA (2016) data, in 2014–2015 over one-half million students played high-school basketball. A small number, 18,697, went on to play college ball at the Division I, II, or III level (National Collegiate Athletic Association 2016). That's 3.5 percent. Based on this number, Kris succeeded. How does one teach for transfer when vital prior knowledge about recirculation is absent? To use Yancey, Robertson, and Taczak's term, how do you *remix* if you don't have an initial mix? Again, here may be a case in which the curricular knowledge Kris received in FYC may have eventually informed his extracurricular knowledge. Maybe by learning how to align his voice with others in his essay, he could have learned to align his body with others on the court. Instead of juxtaposing prior and current knowledge, we were working with concurrent knowledge in which the two flowed together, ideally to form, and reform, Kris as a literate person.

But he is gone.

But if granted another year, just another semester, with Kris, I would strive to help him see how he is caught in vast network of ideas—that the story he has to tell, the arguments he wants to make, are always already entangled in ongoing conversations. If I could get him to see that, maybe I could still watch him play ball. Maybe he would still be on the team instead of . . . I don't know where.

He is gone. Though I have a new group of twenty-plus student-athletes to work closely with this semester, I think of Kris as I make the walk from my office to the classroom, passing the basketball gym on the way.

Isn't it the students we let down who sometimes stick with us the most?

THE FINAL MINUTES OF PLAY

I came not to pen a panegyric to college sports—nor a screed. I came to understand how college sports help compositionists better understand text and how our one-half million student-athletes use text for their sports. Three questions formed my throughline in this book: what are plays and what do they do? How do student-athletes learn plays? And, based on the answers to the first two questions, how can we better teach student-athlete writers? By offering three interconnected questions, I move from understanding how text and student-athletes operate in tandem to how we can leverage this understanding in any writing-intensive space. Two origin stories fueled my entry point to these questions. The first story was about Trey, the highly recruited wide receiver who struggled to compose his success-strategies paper and whose paired joy/frustration with Notepad started my thinking about student-athlete literacy over a decade ago. I moved from the plains of Alabama to the plains of Oklahoma and now to the foothills of the Appalachian Mountains in search of the hows, whys, and whats regarding student-athletes, writing, and literacy. Trey was the lodestar guiding my exploration. I remember the last time I saw him. It was after an Auburn home football game. My wife and I hung around the stadium waiting to greet some players who were in my class. Trey, with his large infectious smile, hugged my wife, shook my hand, and turned and faded into the crowd and out of my research, as he shortly thereafter withdrew from Auburn. I wish I could say I saw him again and could report on his progress. Doing so would add a tidy conclusion and bookend the introduction. But I cannot. Even with the additional Googling that came with writing this book, I couldn't locate him. The lodestar is missing from the horizon, but the journey of better understanding our student-athlete writers continues. At the close, my thoughts are with Trey, that blue-and-orange-and-white Auburn Tiger jersey obscured by the blue-and-orange-and-white-clad fans. With a gracious nod to Trey, I end this book as an initial step toward helping us bring him—and the one-half million other student-athletes—back into our focus. And I firmly believe that bringing our student-athletes into focus begins with a study of the writing practices of our student-athletes.

Notes

1. Small portions of this chapter appear in my article "Student-Athletes, Prior Knowledge, and Threshold Concepts," which was published in *Teaching English in the Two-Year College* (Rifenburg 2016b).

2. For work extending jazz improvisation to teacher-training programs, see Keith Sawyer (2004a; 2004b). For application to writing center work, see Boquet and Eodice (2008), which I engage with more directly in this chapter.

3. I need to acknowledge an important distinction between jazz and athletics: jazz improvisation does not rely on scripted text; college sports do. However, the cognitive moves behind learning and executing the two are remarkably similar, and often coaches use plays to mold performance, not mirror performance. In other words, as Faulkner told me, scripted plays function as "frameworks" for action, and he does not seek to dictate each individual player movement within this framework.

4. Paul Lynch (2013) reminds us that Quintilian, despite his thorough curriculum in *Institutes of Oratory*, wrote, "Let no one demand from me a rigid code of rules such as most authors of textbooks have laid down, or ask me to impose on students of rhetoric a system of laws as immutable as fate" (2). In *The Everyday Writing Center*, Anne Ellen Geller, Michele Eodice, Frankie Condon, Meg Carroll, and Elizabeth H. Boquet also state their hesitation with providing pedagogical directives applicable to a wide variety of learning contexts. Writing almost two thousand years after Quintilian, they argue, "There is no syllabus [in our writing centers], no textbooks; in fact, we warn against the over-reliance on textbooks which can reify memes and mental models—those models which contain rather than expand practice" (Geller et al. 2007, 12).

REFERENCES

Adler, Patricia, and Peter Adler. 1991. *Backboards and Blackboards: College Athletes and Role Engulfment.* New York: Columbia University Press.

Anson, Chris. 2016. "The Pop Warner Chronicle: A Case Study in Contextual Adaptation and the Transfer of Writing Ability." *College Composition and Communication* 67 (4): 518–49.

Baker, Ray Stannard. 1927. *Woodrow Wilson Life & Letters: Princeton, 1890–1910.* New York: Doubleday.

Banks, Adam. 2015. "Ain't No Walls behind the Sky, Baby! Funk, Flight, Freedom." *College Composition and Communication* 67 (2): 267–79.

Barrett, Frank. 1998. "Coda—Creativity and Improvisation in Jazz and Organizations: Implications for Organizational Learning." *Organization Science* 9 (5): 605–21. https://doi.org/10.1287/orsc.9.5.605.

Bazerman, Charles, and Paul Prior, eds. 2004. *What Writing Does and How It Does It.* Mahwah, NJ: Lawrence Erlbaum.

Beaufort, Anne. 2007. *College Writing and Beyond: A New Framework for University Writing Instruction.* Logan: Utah State University Press.

Bell, Lydia F. 2009. "Examining Academic Role-Set Influence on the Student-Athlete Experience." Special issue, *Journal of Intercollegiate Athletics* 19–41. http://csri-jiia.org/old/documents/publications/special_issues/2009/sp_02_Making_of_the_Athlete-Student.pdf.

Berkowitz, Steve, Jodi Upton, and Erik Brady. 2013. "Most NCAA Division I Athletic Departments Take Subsidies." *USA Today,* July 1. https://www.usatoday.com/story/sports/college/2013/05/07/ncaa-finances-subsidies/2142443/.

Berlin, James. 1988. "Rhetoric and Ideology in the Writing Class." *College English* 50 (5): 477–94. https://doi.org/10.2307/377477.

Berliner, Paul F. 1994. *Thinking in Jazz: The Infinite Art of Improvisation.* Chicago: Chicago University Press. https://doi.org/10.7208/chicago/9780226044521.001.0001.

Bitzel, Alanna. 2012. "Supporting Student-Athletes." *Praxis: A Writing Center Journal* 9 (1). http://www.praxisuwc.com/supporting-student-athletes-91.

Bitzer, Lloyd F. 1968. "The Rhetorical Situation." *Philosophy & Rhetoric* 1:1–14.

Bizzell, Patricia. 2014. "We Want to Know Who Our Students Are." *PMLA* 129 (3): 442–47. https://doi.org/10.1632/pmla.2014.129.3.442.

Boquet, Elizabeth H. 2002. *Noise from the Writing Center.* Logan: Utah State University Press.

Boquet, Elizabeth H., and Michele Eodice. 2008. "Creativity in the Writing Center: A Terrifying Conundrum." In *Creative Approaches to Writing Center Work,* edited by Kevin Dvorak and Shanti Bruce, 3–21. Cresskill, NJ: Hampton.

Bragdon, Henry Wilkinson. 1967. *Woodrow Wilson: The Academic Years.* Cambridge, MA: Belknap. https://doi.org/10.4159/harvard.9780674733954.

Brands, H. W. 1997. *T. R.: The Last Romantic.* New York: Basic Books.

Bransford, John D., James W. Pellegrino, and M. Suzanne Donovan, eds. 2000. *How People Learn: Brain, Mind, Experience, and School: Expanded Edition.* Washington, D.C.: National Academy Press.

Broussard, William. 2004. "Writing into the Bounds: Countering the 'Balkanization' of College Athletes." *IWCA Update* 5 (1): 11–15.

Bruner, Jerome. 1978. "The Role of Dialogue in Language Acquisition." In *The Child's Conception of Language,* edited by Anne Sinclair, R. J. Jarvella, and William J. M. Levelt, 241–56. New York: Springer-Verlag.

DOI: 10.7330/9781607326892.c006

Burke, Kenneth. 1973. *The Philosophy of Literary Form: Studies in Symbolic Action.* Berkeley: University of California Press.

Cheville, Julie. 2001. *Minding the Body: What Student-Athletes Know About Learning.* Portsmouth, NH: Heinemann.

Clotfelter, Charles T. 2011. *Big-Time Sports in American Universities.* Cambridge: Cambridge University Press. https://doi.org/10.1017/CBO9780511976902.

Collier, James Lincoln. 1993. *Jazz: The American Theme Song.* New York: Oxford University Press.

Connors, Robert J. 1997. *Composition-Rhetoric: Backgrounds, Theory, and Pedagogy.* Pittsburgh, PA: University of Pittsburgh Press. https://doi.org/10.2307/j.ctt5hjt92.

Csikszentmihalyi, Mihaly. 1998. *Flow: The Psychology of Optimal Experience.* New York: Harper.

CWPA, NCTE, and NWP. 2011. *Framework for Success in Postsecondary Writing.* Council of Writing Program Administrators, National Council of Teachers of English, and National Writing Project. January. http://wpacouncil.org/framework.

Dalton, Kathleen. 2002. *Theodore Roosevelt: A Strenuous Life.* New York: Alfred A. Knopf.

Das, Proloy K. 2000. "Offensive Protection: The Potential Application of Intellectual Property Law to Scripted Sports Plays." *Indiana Law Journal* 75 (3): article 7.

Davis, Miles, with Quincy Troupe. 1989. *Miles: The Autobiography.* New York: Simon & Schuster.

DelliCarpini, Dominic. 2013. "CCCC Secretary's Report 2013–2014." *Conference on College Composition and Communication* 65 (2): 374–78.

Dressman, Mark, Sarah McCarthey, and Paul Prior. 2012. "Editor's Introduction: Literate Practices are Situated, Mediated, Multisemiotic, and Embodied." *Research in the Teaching of English* 47 (1): 5–8.

Elon University. 2013. "Elon Statement on Writing Transfer." http://www.elon.edu/docs/e-web/academics/teaching/ers/writing_transfer/Elon-Statement-Writing-Transfer.pdf.

Eodice, Michele, Steve Price, and Kerri Jordan. 2014. "From the Editors." *Writing Center Journal* 33 (2): 11–14.

Fishman, Jenn, Andrea Lunsford, Beth McGregor, and Mark Otuteye. 2005. "Performing Writing, Performing Literacy." *College Composition and Communication* 57 (2): 224–52.

Fleckenstein, Kristie S. 1999. "Writing Bodies: Somatic Mind in Composition Studies." *College English* 61 (3): 281–306. https://doi.org/10.2307/379070.

Forrester, Scott. 2014. *The Benefits of Campus Recreation.* Corvallis, OR: NIRSA: National Intramural-Recreational Sports Association. http://rfc.wayne.edu/mort-harris/forrester_2014-report.pdf.

Ganim, Sara. 2015. "NCAA: It's Not Our Job to Ensure Educational Quality." CNN.com. http://www.cnn.com/2015/04/01/sport/ncaa-response-to-lawsuit/.

Geller, Anne Ellen, Michele Eodice, Frankie Condon, Meg Carroll, and Elizabeth H. Boquet. 2007. *The Everyday Writing Center: A Community of Practice.* Logan: Utah State University Press. https://doi.org/10.2307/j.ctt4cgmkj.

Giddens, Gary, and Scott DeVeaux. 2009. *Jazz.* New York: Norton.

Gilje, Øystein. 2010. "Multimodal Redesign in Filmmaking Practices: An Inquiry of Young Filmmakers' Deployment of Semiotic Tools in Their Filmmaking Practice." *Written Communication* 27 (4): 494–522. https://doi.org/10.1177/0741088310377874.

Gorzelsky, Gwen, Dana Lynn Driscoll, Joe Paszek, Ed Jones, and Carol Hayes. 2017. "Cultivating Constructive Metacognition: A New Taxonomy for Writing Studies." In *Critical Transitions: Writing and the Question of Transfer,* edited by Chris M. Anson and Jessie L. Moore, 215–46. Fort Collins, CO: WAC Clearinghouse.

Grant-Davie, Keith. 1997. "Rhetorical Situations and Their Constituents." *Rhetoric Review* 15 (2): 264–79. https://doi.org/10.1080/07350199709359219.

Gries, Laurie E. 2013. "Iconographic Tracking: A Digital Research Method for Visual Rhetoric and Circulation Studies." *Computers and Composition* 30 (4): 332–48. https://doi.org/10.1016/j.compcom.2013.10.006.

Gries, Laurie E. 2015. *Still Life with Rhetoric: A New Materialist Approach to Visual Rhetorics.* Logan: Utah State University Press.

Grutsch McKinney, Jackie. 2013. *Peripheral Visions for Writing Center Work.* Logan: Utah State University Press. https://doi.org/10.2307/j.ctt4cgk97.

Harris, Joseph. 2006. *Rewriting: How to Do Things with Text.* Logan: Utah State University Press.

Harris, Joseph. 2012. *A Teaching Subject: Composition Since 1966.* Logan: Utah State University Press. https://doi.org/10.2307/j.ctt4cgrgw.

Hassel, Holly, and Joanne Baird Giordano. 2013. "Occupy Writing Studies: Rethinking College Composition for the Needs of the Teaching Majority." *College Composition and Communication* 65 (1): 117–40.

Hawhee, Debra. 2004. *Bodily Arts: Rhetoric and Athletics in Ancient Greece.* Austin: University of Texas Press.

Hayes, Hogan, Dana Ferris, and Carl Whithaus. 2017. "Dynamic Transfer in First Year Writing and WID Settings." In *Critical Transitions: Writing and the Question of Transfer,* edited by Chris M. Anson and Jessie L. Moore, 181–215. Fort Collins, CO: WAC Clearinghouse.

Hutchins, Edwin. 1995. *Cognition in the Wild.* Cambridge, MA: MIT Press.

Iedema, Rick. 2001. "Resemiotization." *Semiotica* 37 (1–4): 23–39.

Iedema, Rick. 2003. "Multimodality, Resemiotization: Extending the Analysis of Discourse as Multi-Semiotic Practice." *Visual Communication* 2 (1): 29–57. https://doi.org/10.11 77/1470357203002001751.

Indiana University Bloomington Center for Postsecondary Research. 2015. "Beginning College Survey of Student Engagement." *BCSSE Summary Report.* Bloomington: Indiana University Center for Postsecondary Research. http://bcsse.indiana.edu/pdf/2015/BC SSE15%20Summary%20Report-Grand.pdf.

Isaacs, Emily, and Melissa Knight. 2014. "A Bird's Eye View of Writing Centers: Institutional Infrastructure, Scope and Programmatic Issues, Reported Practices." *WPA: Writing Program Administration* 37 (2): 36–67.

Isocrates. 1929. *Antidosis.* Vol 2. Translator George Norlin. Loeb Classical Library, 179–367. Cambridge: Harvard University Press.

Johnson, Mark. 1987. *The Body in the Mind: The Bodily Basis of Meaning, Imagination, and Reason.* Chicago: Chicago University Press.

Kieff, F. F. Scott, Robert G. Kramer, and Robert M. Kunstadt. 2008. "It's Your Turn, But It's My Move: Intellectual Property Protection for Sports Moves." *Santa Clara High Technology Law Journal* 25 (4): 765–85.

Killingsworth, M. Jimmie, and Michael K. Gilbertson. 1992. *Signs, Genres, and Communication in Technical Communication.* New York: Baywood.

Knoblauch, A. Abby. 2012. "Bodies of Knowledge: Definitions, Delineations, and Implications of Embodied Writing in the Academy." *Composition Studies* 40 (2): 50–65.

Kress, Gunther. 2010. *Multimodality: A Social Semiotic Approach to Contemporary Communication.* London: Routledge.

Kroll, Barry M. 2013. *The Open Hand: Arguing as an Art of Peace.* Logan: Utah State University Press. https://doi.org/10.2307/j.ctt4cgnz9.

Kuh, George D. 2008. *High-Impact Educational Practices: What They Are, Who Has Access to Them, and Why They Matter.* Washington, DC: American Association of Colleges and Universities.

Latour, Bruno. 2006. *Reassembling the Social: An Introduction to Actor-Network Theory.* New York: Oxford University Press.

Layden, Tim. 2010. *Blood, Sweat, and Chalk: The Ultimate Football Playbook: How the Great Coaches Built Today's Game.* New York: Sports Illustrated Books.

Lerner, Neal. 1998. "Drill Pads, Teaching Machines, and Programmed Texts: Origins of Instructional Technology in Writing Centers." In *Wiring the Writing Center,* edited by Eric H. Hobson, 119–36. Logan: Utah State University Press. https://doi.org/10.2307/j.ctt 46nzf8.12.

Lester, Robin. 1999. *Stagg's University: The Rise, Decline, and Fall of Big-Time Football at Chicago.* Chicago: University of Illinois Press.

Lucas, Christopher J. 1994. *American Higher Education: A History.* New York: St. Martin's.

Lunsford, Andrea A. 2006. "Writing, Technologies, and the Fifth Canon." *Computers and Composition* 23 (2): 169–77. https://doi.org/10.1016/j.compcom.2006.02.002.

Lynch, Paul. 2013. *After Pedagogy: The Experience of Teaching.* Urbana, IL: NCTE.

Malafouris, Lambros. 2013. *How Things Shape the Mind: A Theory of Material Engagement.* Cambridge: MIT Press.

Malenczyk, Rita, ed. 2013. *A Rhetoric for Writing Program Administrators.* Anderson, SC: Parlor Press.

Marrou, H. I. 1982. *A History of Education in Antiquity.* Translator George Lamb. Madison: University of Wisconsin Press.

McCants, Rashanda, and Devon Ramsay v. The National Collegiate Athletic Association and The University of North Carolina at Chapel Hill. 2015. Durham County (North Carolina) Superior Court. January 22. https://www.washingtonpost.com/news/grade-point/wp -content/uploads/sites/42/2015/01/UNC-Complaint-Filed-Copy-1-22-15.pdf.

Micciche, Laura. 2014. "Writing Material." *College English* 76 (6): 488–505.

Miller, John J. 2011. *The Big Scrum: How Teddy Roosevelt Saved Football.* New York: Harper.

Moberg, Brent C. 2004. "Football Play Scripts: A Potential Pitfall for Federal Copyright Law?" *Marquette Sports Law Review* 14 (2): 525–50.

Moll, Luis, and Norma González. 2001. "Lessons from Research with Language-Minority Children." In *Literacy: A Critical Sourcebook,* edited by Ellen Cushman, Eugene R. Kintgen, Barry M. Kroll, and Mike Rose, 156–71. Boston, MA: Bedford/St. Martin's.

Naismith, James. 1941. *Basketball: Its Origin and Development.* New York: Association Press.

National Center for Education Statistics. 2010. "Classification of Instructional Programs." https://nces.ed.gov/ipeds/cipcode/Default.aspx?y=55.

National Center for Education Statistics. 2017. *Digest of Education Statistics.* https://nces .ed.gov/fastfacts/display.asp?id=372.

National Collegiate Athletic Association. 2016. "Probability of Competing beyond High School."http://www.ncaa.org/about/resources/research/probability-competing -beyond-high-School.

National Collegiate Athletic Association. 2017a. *2017–2018 NCAA Division I Manual.* https://www.ncaapublications.com/p-4511-2017-2018-ncaa-division-i-manual-august -version-available-august-2017.aspx.

National Collegiate Athletic Association. 2017b. *NCAA Sports Sponsorship and Participation Rates Report: Student-Athlete Participation, 1981/82–2016/17.* http://www.ncaa.org/sites /default/files/2016-17NCAA-0472_ParticRatesReport-FINAL_20171120.pdf.

National Collegiate Athletics Association and Subsidiaries. 2015. https://www.ncaa.org/sites /default/files/2014-15NCAA_Financial_Statement.pdf.

National Council of Teachers of English. 2004. "NCTE Beliefs about the Teaching of Writing." Writing Study Group of the NCTE Executive Committee. http://www2.ncte.org /statements//writingbeliefs.

National Council of Teachers of English. 2015. "CCCC Guidelines for the Ethical Conduct of Research in Composition Studies." http://cccc.ncte.org/cccc/resources/positions /ethicalconduct. First published in 2003; revised in 2015.

National Federation of High School Associations. 2015. "2014–2015 High School Athletics Participation Survey Results." http://www.nfhs.org/ParticipationStatics/PDF/2014 -15_Participation_Survey_Results.pdf.

Nelson, Jane, and Margaret Garner. 2011. "Horizontal Structures for Learning." In *Before and After the Tutorial: Writing Centers and Institutional Relationships,* edited by Nicholas Mauriello, William J. Macauley, and Robert T. Koch, 7–27. Creskill, NJ: Hampton.

New London Group. 1996. "A Pedagogy of Multiliteracies: Designing Social Futures." *Harvard Educational Review* 66 (1): 60–92. https://doi.org/10.17763/haer.66.1.17370n67v22j160u.

North, Stephen. 1984. "The Idea of a Writing Center." *College English* 46 (5): 433–46.

Perry, Kathryn. 2012. "The Movement of Composition: Dance and Writing." *Kairos: A Journal of Rhetoric, Technology, and Pedagogy.* 17 (1). http://kairos.technorhetoric.net /17.1/disputatio/perry/.

Pope, Edwin. 1955. *Football's Greatest Coaches.* New York: Tupper and Love.

Powel, Harford. 2008. *Walter Camp: The Father of American Football.* Freeport, NY: Books for Libraries Press. First published in 1926.

Prior, Paul. 1998. *Writing/Disciplinarity: A Sociohistoric Account of Literate Activity in the Academy.* Mahwah, NJ: Lawrence Erlbaum.

Puntambekar, Sadhana, and Roland Hübscher. 2005. "Tools for Scaffolding Students in a Complex Learning Environment: What Have We Gained and What Have We Missed?" *Educational Psychologist* 40 (1): 1–12. https://doi.org/10.1207/s15326985ep4001_1.

Reynolds, Nedra. 2004. *Geographies of Writing: Inhabiting Places and Encountering Difference.* Carbondale: Southern Illinois University Press.

Rifenburg, J. Michael. 2014. "Writing as Embodied, College Football Plays as Embodied: Extracurricular Multimodal Composing." *Composition Forum* 29. http://compositionfo rum.com/issue/29/writing-as-embodied.php.

Rifenburg, J. Michael. 2016a. "The Literate Practices of a Division II Men's Basketball Team." *Grassroots Writing Research Journal* 6 (2): 55–63.

Rifenburg, J. Michael. 2016b. "Student-Athletes, Prior Knowledge, and Threshold Concepts." *Teaching English in the Two-Year College* 44 (1): 32–48.

Rifenburg, J. Michael. 2016c. "Supporting the Student-Athlete Writer: A Case Study of a Division I Athletics Writing Centers and NCAA Academic Mandates." *Writing Center Journal* 35 (2): 61–87. writingcenterjournal.org.

Ritter, Kelly. 2013. "Who Are Students?" In *A Rhetoric for Writing Program Administrators,* edited by Rita Malenczyk, 11–23. Anderson, SC: Parlor.

Roozen, Kevin. 2008. "Journalism, Poetry, Stand-Up Comedy, and Academic Literacy: Mapping the Interplay of Curricular and Extracurricular Literate Activities." *Journal of Basic Writing* 27 (1): 5–34.

Roozen, Kevin. 2009. "From Journals to Journalism: Tracing Trajectories of Literate Development." *College Composition and Communication* 60 (3): 541–53.

Rudolph, Frederick. 1968. *The American College and University: A History.* New York: Alfred A. Knopf.

Sawyer, Keith. 1992. "Improvisational Creativity: An Analysis of Jazz Performance." *Creativity Research Journal* 5 (3): 253–63. https://doi.org/10.1080/10400419209534439.

Sawyer, Keith. 2004a. "Creative Teaching: Collaborative Discussion as Disciplined Improvisation." *Educational Review* 33 (2): 12–20.

Sawyer, Keith. 2004b. "Improvised Lessons: Collaborative Discussion in the Constructivist Classroom." *Teaching Education* 15 (2): 189–201. https://doi.org/10.1080/104762104 2000213610.

Shipka, Jody. 2011. *Toward a Composition Made Whole.* Pittsburg, PA: Pittsburg University Press. https://doi.org/10.2307/j.ctt5hjqkk.

Smith, Chris. 2014. "College Football's Most Valuable Teams 2014." *Forbes,* December 22. https://www.forbes.com/sites/chrissmith/2014/12/22/college-footballs-most-valu able-teams-2014/2/.

Smith, Chris. 2015. "College Basketball's Most Valuable Teams: Louisville on Top, Kansas Close Behind." *Forbes,* March 16. https://www.forbes.com/sites/chrissmith/2015/03/16/ college-basketballs-most-valuable-teams-louisville-on-top-kansas-close-behind/.

Smith, Ronald A. 1990. *Sports and Freedom: The Rise of Big-Time College Athletics.* New York: Oxford University Press.

Solomon, Jon. 2015. "How Long Is Too Long a College Football Game?" CBSSports.com. February 9. https://www.cbssports.com/collegefootball/writer/jon-solomon/25063815 /how-long-is-too-long-a-college-football-game.

Sperber, Murray. 1990. *College Sports Inc.: The Athletic Department vs. the University.* New York: Henry Holt.

Sperber, Murray. 2000. *Beer and Circus: How Big-Time College Sports Is Crippling Undergraduate Education.* New York: Henry Holt.

Stagg, Amos Alonzo, and Wesley Winons Stout. 1927. *Touchdown!* New York: Longman's.

Syverson, Margaret. 1999. *The Wealth of Reality: An Ecology of Composition.* Carbondale: Southern Illinois University Press.

Thelin, John R. 1994. *Games Colleges Play: Scandal and Reform in Intercollegiate Athletics.* Baltimore, MD: Johns Hopkins University Press.

Thelin, John R. 2004. *A History of American Higher Education.* Baltimore, MD: Johns Hopkins University Press.

Thompson, Isabelle. 2009. "Scaffolding in the Writing Center: A Microanalysis of an Experienced Tutor's Verbal and Nonverbal Tutoring Strategies." *Written Communication* 26 (4): 417–53. https://doi.org/10.1177/0741088309342364.

Tinberg, Howard. 2015. "Metacognition Is Not Cognition." In *Naming What We Know: Threshold Concepts in Writing Studies,* edited by Linda Adler-Kassner and Elizabeth Wardle, 75–77. Logan: Utah State University Press.

Tracey, Jill, and John Corlett. 1995. "The Transition Experience of First-Year University Track and Field Student Athletes." *Journal of the Freshman Year Experience* 7 (2): 82–102.

University of Oklahoma. 2018. Oklahoma Compliance Mission and Vision Statements. http://www.soonersports.com/fls/31000/old_site/pdf/genrel/20090611_compliance_mission.pdf?DB_OEM_ID=31000.

University of Oklahoma Department of Intercollegiate Athletics. 2015. *Annual Report 2014–2015.* https://admin.xosn.com/pdf9/4325007.pdf?DB_OEM_ID=31000&.

Vygotsky, Lev. 1978. *Mind in Society: The Development of Higher Psychological Processes.* Cambridge: Harvard University Press.

Wainstein, Kenneth, A. Joseph Jay, and Colleen Depman Kukowski. 2014. "Investigation of Irregular Classes in the Department of African and Afro-American Studies at the University of North Carolina at Chapel Hill." October 22. https://carolinacommitment.unc.edu/files/2014/10/UNC-FINAL-REPORT.pdf.

Wardle, Elizabeth, and Doug Downs, eds. 2014. *Writing about Writing. Boston.* Bedford, MA: St. Martin's.

White, Edward M., Norbert Elliot, and Irvin Peckham. 2015. *Very Like a Whale: The Assessment of Writing Programs.* Logan: Utah State University Press.

Witte, Stephen. 1992. "Context, Text, and Intertext: Toward a Constructivist Semiotic of Writing." *Written Communication* 9 (2): 237–308. https://doi.org/10.1177/0741088392009002003.

Wolverton, Brad. 2012. "The Education of Dasmine Cathey." *Chronicle of Higher Education,* June 8. http://chronicle.com/interactives/dasmine-cathey.

Yancey, Kathleen Blake. 2008. "The Impulse to Compose and the Age of Composition." *Research in the Teaching of English* 43 (3): 316–38.

Yancey, Kathleen Blake. 2014. "A Mixed Genre—Locations of Writing; (Another Beginning), Another Farewell." *College Composition and Communication* 66 (2): 213–21.

Yancey, Kathleen Blake, ed. 2016. *A Rhetoric of Reflection.* Logan: Utah State University Press.

Yancey, Kathleen Blake, Liane Robertson, and Kara Taczak. 2014. *Writing across Contexts: Transfer, Composition, and Sites of Writing.* Logan: Utah State University Press. https://doi.org/10.2307/j.ctt6wrr95.

Yost, Mark. 2010. *Varsity Green: A Behind the Scenes Look at Culture and Corruption in College Athletics.* Stanford, CA: Stanford University Press.

Zimbalist, Andrew. 1990. *Unpaid Professionals: Commercialism and Conflict in Big-Time College Sports.* Princeton: Princeton University Press.

ABOUT THE AUTHOR

J. MICHAEL RIFENBURG is an associate professor in the English Department at the University of North Georgia where he directors the First-Year Composition Program and is Faculty Fellow for Scholarly Writing in UNG's Center for Teaching, Learning, and Leadership. After coaching high-school soccer and teaching high-school literature, he turned to working with student-athletes at the Division I and II levels. With Patricia Portanova and Duane Roen, he coedited *Contemporary Perspectives on Cognition and Writing* (WAC Clearinghouse, 2017). He tweets writing, sports, and beer @jmrifenburg.

INDEX

Page numbers in italics indicate illustrations.